ST MARTIN'S

The Making of a Masterpiece

Arthur Penn

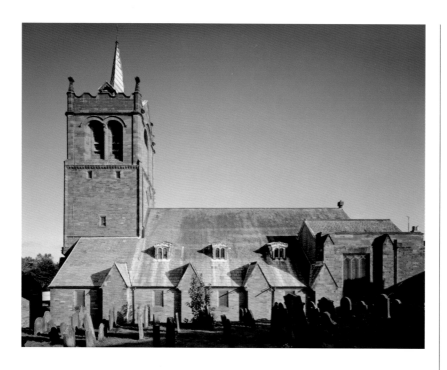

Main text set in Bembo, headings set in Spectrum

ISBN 978-0-9559175-0-9

Published by David Penn at millyardstudios.co.uk
Printed by Shanleys
Designed by Mullin Design

ST MARTIN'S
The Making of a Masterpiece

Arthur Penn

FOREWORD

The text of this book was written fourteen years ago as a contribution to a restoration appeal for St Martin's. It was produced economically and without coloured illustrations which at that time would have added prohibitively to the cost of production. Now a reprint is called for and it is possible to match the text with excellent illustrations. Sonia Halliday photographed the windows in 1977 and she has kindly agreed that her photographs should be used. Sheila Kirk's splendid book on Philip Webb was published in 2005 and she and her photographer Martin Charles have agreed to the use of some of their illustrations. It has also been possible to make corrections and incorporate some additional information in a completely new edition. I am very grateful to my son, David, for producing the new edition.

As Vicar of St Martin's between 1967 and 1983 I worshipped day by day and week by week in this lovely building. I was able to study the well-preserved archive of the church's building, to see its context in Victorian church architecture and to learn about the Morris firm and its output of stained glass. I received help from many visitors with special knowledge, including Sheila Kirk, John Brandon Jones, Leonard Evetts, Peter Cormack and David O'Connor, many of whom became friends as well as advisers. So it became possible to construct a detailed account of the church, its building, its stained glass and the remarkable people who created it. Not all were devout churchmen but all believed in their varying ways that this house of God should be a worthy contribution to the art of its period and a valuable feature of the town of Brampton.

The appreciation of church buildings in our country has been enriched in recent decades by the writings of Nikolaus Pevsner, John Betjeman and Simon Jenkins. Pevsner's study of the buildings of England has taught us all a lot about our churches and it was he who in 1967 drew the attention of a wider public to St Martin's. John Betjeman claimed Philip Webb was an atheist, a term Webb did not accept, but Betjeman's appreciation was that of a believing Christian who understood and valued what went on in churches. Jenkins's appreciation is quite different. He objected to church guides that claimed a church was not a museum but a place of worship. He said we should be proud that our churches are museums and claimed not to understand TS Eliot's words in *Little Gidding*:

> You are not here to verify,
> Instruct yourself, inform curiosity
> Or carry report. You are here to kneel
> Where prayer has been valid.

However, after his study of 'the best thousand' churches he felt, with Philip Larkin, bidden 'to take off my cycle clips in awkward reverence.'

This contrast expresses the problem of the parish church in England in the early 21st Century. We have failed to stem the reduction in church going and perhaps in Christian belief, yet more and more people without such belief value our churches and support their maintenance.

As a parish priest for 38 years, an auxiliary minister in retirement for 20 more, and an honorary canon of Carlisle Cathedral, I shared in the care of some 15 churches. Some of those buildings were not outstanding, though all were worthy, and I discovered that a parish clergyman is not only a pastor and preacher but also a curator. Some clergy almost resent this role, but I found it rewarding. Before coming to Brampton, I had the care of an outstanding pre-conquest church, St Gregory's Minster, Kirkdale in Yorkshire for twelve years. I studied Anglo-Saxon art and architecture to understand it. Then I came to Brampton and found a relatively modern but equally unique church; not what Jenkins would call 'a gallery of vernacular art' (though Webb and Morris valued such) but the creation of outstanding modern artists of the late 19th century. Who would not be proud to be such a curator? But I came as a parish priest and worshipper in this building and found it inspiring. I hope and pray that our wonderful buildings will continue to draw both those who will 'kneel where prayer has been valid' and those who come simply to 'verify, instruct themselves, inform curiosity and carry report' and help maintain such houses of prayer, and that this book will help them to do so.

Arthur Penn
February 2008

ST MARTIN'S
The Making of a Masterpiece

CONTENTS

ST MARTIN'S
The Making of a Masterpiece

ILLUSTRATIONS

INTRODUCTION

'It is very dark inside and has been spoiled by lurid modern windows which I could only regard as disastrous.' The words of a writer describing a detour to Brampton Church as he tramped Hadrian's Wall in 1956.[1]

Many have thought otherwise and made long journeys to see those windows. When Sir Nikolaus Pevsner wrote his Cumberland and Westmorland volume of *The Buildings of England* in 1967, he described the church as 'a remarkable building'. The east window, he said, 'is glowing with gem-stone colours… What a revolution Morris glass was, with its clarity and intensity… The church is impressive everywhere… The interior has the great asset of beautiful Morris windows.'

In the nineteen fifties the Pre-Raphaelites were out of fashion; since then they have come into their own and, among their other artistic achievements, their stained glass has been recognised as a valuable part of our artistic heritage. When Charles Sewter published his *Stained Glass of William Morris and his Circle* in two large volumes in 1974 and 1975, the scale of that achievement became apparent. Significantly, a photograph of the Brampton East Window adorned the dust cover of volume 1. Literally hundreds of churches, as well as a few houses and public buildings, have examples, and a few, like St Martin's Scarborough, Selsley in Gloucestershire, Middleton Cheney in Northamptonshire and Allerton, in Liverpool, have extensive sets of windows by William Morris's company. Brampton is another, with as many as fourteen. But what makes Brampton unique is not merely the quantity and quality of its windows, but also the fact that its architect, Philip Webb, was one of that same circle of artists and one of the original seven partners in 'the Firm'. As a result the whole conception is an integrated one.

EARLIER CHURCHES

It was on St Martin's Day, 11th November 1878, that Bishop Harvey Goodwin consecrated the present church. Brampton had, however, already had a church for at least a thousand years. Indeed, there was probably a church before there was a Brampton, but it was a little way away. Old Church, as it is known, a mile and a half to the west, was the site of church and parsonage until the late 18th Century. The old church itself, the chancel of which remains, lies in the site of a Roman fort, one of a series lying along the Stanegate, constructed before the building of Hadrian's Wall. There is every reason to suppose that it came into existence in the years following the Roman withdrawal and to connect it with the mission initiated by St Ninian. Rebuilt in the Norman period it survived until the parishioners petitioned the Earl of Carlisle to replace it with a church in the town in 1778. The reasons for such a long delay in the provision of a church in the market town would appear to be threefold. The first was the long period of Border warfare, which reduced the market town, despite having been granted a charter by Henry III in 1252, to a tiny village. The second was the fact that the man who refounded Brampton and obtained a new market charter from James I, Lord William Howard, known as 'Belted Will', was a Roman Catholic. The third was the fact that his descendant, the 2nd Earl of Carlisle, who proposed such a town church, was disgusted by the lack of enthusiasm of the vicar, Philip Fielding and, instead of a church, built an almshouse in the town in 1688. Brampton Hospital, as it was called, comprised a number of one-room dwellings for the aged, a chapel and a small grammar school, but due to problems with its endowment, it faded out in the early 19th Century. Meanwhile, understandably enough, Brampton parishioners had found its chapel a more convenient place of worship than Old Church, and by 1749 it is recorded by Chancellor Waugh that 'the service, except the first Sunday in the month, is performed in a decent chapel made out of the hospital.'

The 1778 project was to demolish the Old Church, except for the chancel, which was to be retained for use at funerals, and to use the stone to convert part of the hospital into a church. It seems to have been a very half-hearted effort, resulting in a curious building with the altar on the long south side. It was enlarged to take in the rest of the hospital in 1828, when a tower was built to take the two ancient bells and four others given by the vicar, Thomas Ramshay. The cost of the enlargement was £1800.

The building seems never to have attracted the love of its parishioners. Later, Canon Rawnsley described it as 'a mean-looking structure, having common sash windows. Its only redeeming feature was its tower. It wanted re-seating, and a great deal needed to be done, as it was much out of repair from damp and other causes.' Bishop Goodwin spoke likewise of a church 'the disappearance of which I should suppose few, if any, will regret. In truth it was a very unhappy specimen of church building. I remember well and sadly the impression it made upon my mind when I first saw it and officiated in it… a church in presence of which it would have been hard to say 'How amiable is thy dwelling place, O Lord of hosts'. These words would have stuck in the throat. A church which sinned too in more respects than want of beauty, because it was so utterly inconvenient for the church's services; it seemed as if it had been built by someone who did not know the exact purposes for which his building would be used. So far as external conditions can freeze the warm lifeblood of the soul, that church appeared calculated to do it.' Charles Howard gave a similar verdict. 'In all my experience I never saw a church of a meaner character or less worthy of its object.' Like most churches of its time it was filled with pews, appropriated by the more affluent parishioners. Faculties for sittings (recording these rights) in 1789, and again after the 1828 enlargement, are among the parish records.

Christopher Benson was vicar from 1841 to 1874 and in his time there was a proposal to re-pew the church. An undated poster survives among the parish records, saying:

CHURCH RATE EXTRAORDINARY!

An attempt is to be made by calling a Vestry Meeting to levy a rate on the parishioners for the purpose of re-pewing the Parish Church etc, etc, etc at a probable cost of several hundred pounds. Are the ratepayers aware of this attempt to disturb the peace of the parish and to oppress the Poor? Ratepayers attend! and give it your determined opposition!

Other evidence of this incident is to be found in the poems of Peter Burn, a local poet, draper and congregationalist.[2] A poem in the style of the Ingoldsby Legends and called *The Logic of Crows* is preceded by a note:

Written on the occasion of a Vestry Meeting called to consider the re-pewing of Brampton Parish Church, shortly before the passing of 'The Compulsory Church Rates Abolition Act' in 1868. The Nonconformists overthrew the meeting on the grounds of its being illegal – the notice on the church doors having been within the time specified by Act of Parliament.

The poem is about the birds holding a meeting to discuss 'the making more cosy our much-loved nest' for the benefit of the jackdaws and crows. Here are a few verses of it:

The chairman proposes –
'I think one and all,
Both great bird and small,
Should answer the call
By bringing a feather,
Or something or other,
To help to improve
The place that we love –
Our lofty Crow Hall…'

At this there's a twitter
And scratching of claws;
The twitter most bitter
Is met by 'caws, caws.'
But word-shots 'a hitter'
Are shot at the crows,
Small birds down-twitter
The crows and jackdaws.

Up jumps a little
Despicable sparrow…
'You must think we sparrows
Are semi-rocked fellows –
Are soft-headed things.
We pooh-pooh the movement
The crow-nest improvement…'

But one yellow-hammer
Beat them all hollow;…
'I wish you to know
(And I speak for the rest),
Not a feather shall go
From wing or from breast,
To feather the nest
Of jackdaw or crow…'

And there was much laughing
That day, and much chaffing,
And there was much flapping of wing,
And there was much croaking,
And boisterous talking,
But all was forgot in the spring.

The abolition of Church Rates left the parish in a desperate state. Benson was old and infirm and no new way of raising finance to replace the Church Rate was found. In 1871 the Bishop appointed William Miller as curate in charge because of the vicar's infirmity. He found, he says in an open letter later addressed to the parishioners, 'debt and degradation', with bells unrung and the floors unswept because the ringers and sweepers were on strike for a year's arrears of wages. Miller was typical of the more High Church clergy of the time, who found the whole set-up slovenly and irreverent. He set about reform vigorously and probably insensitively and raised a hornets' nest of opposition. This included a campaign of disruption of the church services led by the organist, the vicar's son, Christopher Benson junior. Miller mentions 'Persistent attempts at disturbance by gestures and noises of contempt and ridicule from the singing gallery'. At length Miller persuaded the churchwardens to threaten Benson junior with a charge of brawling in church if he did not resign. He did so, but when he died 25 years later he was a much respected churchwarden, bank manager and justice of the peace. After two and a half years Benson senior retired and Miller was disappointed in not being appointed in his place – hence his open letter. Instead the patrons, the Trustees of the Earl of Carlisle, appointed Henry Whitehead. Whitehead recognised that Miller had 'broken up a good deal of rough ground' and so prepared the way for radical change.

One of these changes concerned the pews. Whitehead was a born social reformer and a strong antagonist of the whole system of appropriated pews, which made church-going so unattractive to the poor. A printed sermon of his on the subject of free and open churches survives. In it he said: 'it is pleasant to see so many persons here who no matter whether rightly or wrongly, once considered they had no part or lot in their parish church, under a system of appropriated seats.' He must have been determined to rid Brampton of such a system, but his first step was to call a meeting in the Moot Hall 'for the purpose of considering the advisability of re-pewing the Parish Church'. Whitehead grew to love Brampton and its people and came to the conclusion that one should never hurry a meeting of Cumberland men. They will always come to a right decision in the end. Their motto is 'Tak' time'. He hardly followed his own precept in the matter of St Martin's and its pews. He arrived in April 1874 and the Moot Hall meeting was on 22nd June. A committee was appointed to examine the state of the church and it reported to a further meeting on 14th September at the Howard Arms Assembly Room. There a resolution was passed 'that it is desirable that a New Church be built for the parish of Brampton'.

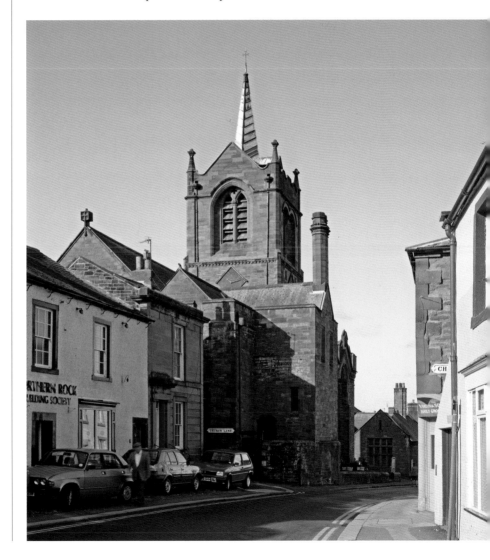

St Martin's Church, looking south west

St Martin's Church,
the nave, looking east

THE BUILDING OF SAINT MARTIN'S

With that meeting on 14th September 1874 the project began. The Hon Charles Howard, brother of the Earl of Carlisle, took the chair, and his son George (together with his wife Rosalind) was also present. Whitehead put the case for a new church. He later admitted in a letter to a friend that there was at first a good deal of passive resistance and 'if I had assumed the attitude of a promoter of it, I daresay it might have fallen to the ground. How I contrived to fan the idea without putting myself into such an attitude I could only explain *viva voce*.' The press report suggests that he took a more positive part. He explained the need for re-pewing and for very heavy repairs and enlargement 'that would cost as much as a new church'. He stated that the Earl's trustees (the estate was administered by a trust during the insanity of the 8th Earl) had offered £2,000 and Mr Charles Howard £500. Major Thompson of Farlam Hall had given £300, Mr GJ Johnson of Castlesteads and Mr George Routledge £100 each. With other promises they already had £3,500 and a cost of something just over £6,000 was envisaged. Dr Armstrong proposed, and Mr Carrick, a local solicitor, seconded the resolution that the church be built, and it was carried unanimously. The committee was transformed from an exploratory one to a building committee. In closing the proceedings Mr Charles Howard mentioned that help would be forthcoming from the estate if a tramway or a sewerage system were planned. These were two much-discussed needs. Miller had campaigned to improve sanitation, as the Brampton Beck which then ran open, was treated as a sewer and receptacle of refuse. Brampton had been by-passed by the railway, mainly for engineering reasons, and linked with it by the 'Dandy' branch line. This ended with the Coal Staithes at the foot of the present Station Road, and it was desired to extend it. A letter appeared in the press at the time of the church proposal suggesting that a tramway was more needed than a church, and a memorial of the parishioners to the Earl's trustees was printed and issued on 31st December 1875 making four suggestions, one of which was a tramway extension.

The statue of the 7th Earl had, a few years earlier, been erected on the Mote[3] and the subscription list for this seems to have been the basis for an appeal for money. A local solicitor, Thomas Forster, was secretary of the committee, and much of his correspondence is preserved in the parish records. An influential member of the committee, though resident in London, was Mr George Routledge, the publisher. He acted as agent in soliciting subscriptions from people in London with a Brampton connection. Whitehead regarded 'Tak' time' as Brampton's motto, but commented that it was due largely to the irresistable energy of a man born and bred in Brampton, George Routledge, who whenever the committee was taking time would descend upon them, that completion came as soon as it did. One of Routledge's letters is particularly interesting as it speaks of his attempt to get a donation from Angela Burdett-Coutts, later a baroness and outstanding philanthropist. It seems that Routledge was disappointed for he wrote, 'She has laid down a strict rule in these matters – she obtained her large fortune from her grandfather Mr Coutts and not from the Duchess of St Albans.'[4]

George Howard not only made a personal donation of £316 but also acted as a fund-raiser. One of the letters he received in response to this appeal is one of astonishing illegibility from the aged Thomas Henry Graham of Edmond Castle. It is revealing in what it tells of how landowners looked on the provision of churches. He begins by telling Howard that it is not in his power to give much. He then recounts his own expenditure on the church and parsonage at Talkin, pointing out that Lord Carlisle also had property in the township. For this he had made provision and marked off three pews for the Earl's family close to the pulpit. He had also been at heavy expense providing a school, with facilities for worship, at the Faugh, and for additions to Carlisle Infirmary, 'so that I am in common parlance very hard up… As to Brampton, I have only about £40 a year annual value in it and only one cottage.' However, as a token of goodwill to the town of Brampton and to Howard's family, he promises £20 'which you must excuse my paying 'til Christmas 1875' (15 months later).

The Trustees of the estate were insistent that their promised contribution was dependent upon their approval of the architect, and it is plain that George Howard's friend Philip Webb was their choice. As early as 4th November Webb sent his report to Forster. Five possible sites had been suggested and Webb gave his views on these:

1 Little's property near the National Schools, which was too much surrounded by the backs of houses and had a bad approach;

2 Smithy Banks which was near a large manufactory with which the

church could not compete in size and the rise and fall of the ground was too rapid;

3 The existing church site;

4 Mounsey's ground at the west end of the church, which would require further purchases and still not give a proper approach;

5 Town Foot which, though freer of objectionable buildings, had nothing else to commend it and would not allow the church to be a marked feature of the town.

Webb thus came down in favour of the existing site, where old materials could be used, which was also central, and where the old graveyard could be protected. The building would hold 500 people, and would be brought to within seven to eight feet of the street boundary and also advanced to the boundaries on the east and west. The floor level would be raised three feet. Prices were given as follows:

Body of church	£5,500
Heating	£200
Clerk of Works	£320
Architect	£300
Travelling	£50
	———
Deduct value of old materials	£300
Add for completion of tower and hanging bells	£775
	———
	£6,845
	———

This report was considered by the committee on 11th November and it was decided to ask Webb to reduce the estimate to £6,000. Charles Howard, who was absent, protested that the architect's plan should not be spoiled by economies, and suggested rather that building should be postponed while more money was raised and interest accumulated. Webb promised plans which would bear in mind the £6,000 maximum. Meanwhile Charles Howard's words bore fruit, for Forster wrote to ask Webb to include in his plans and estimates the difference between the modified and original proposals. George Routledge opposed the limitation to £6,000 and wanted a church which would be an ornament to the town.

Charles Roberts records a story that on his first visit to Naworth in connection with the church, Webb either went away, or proposed to leave next morning, saying there were too many architects. 'I think one sees the committee of Mr and Mrs George Howard, their friends, and perhaps some of the older children all making suggestions.'[5]

On 3rd March 1875 Webb's plans were complete and dispatched to the committee. His design included a fortress-like east end, with a five-light window between projecting blocks of vestry and organ chamber. A rough sketch shows how he saw it from the north-east corner. The road frontage was to consist of three great two-light windows with tracery, each with its own embattled gable. The south side was to have tiny windowless gables, punctuated by small rectangular windows, and with one tiny dormer in the midst of an enormous roof area. At the west he planned an impressive tower, crowned by an octagon and spire. Webb's sketch showed a building standing free, but in fact the church was to be hemmed in by other property on all sides except the 'back' where the little churchyard of the former almshouse provided some space. It is only in recent years that demolition for road improvements has given the church room to be seen as a whole.

The plan of the building was quite unlike most Victorian churches. The body was to be almost square, and although an arcade of four bays paid homage to the Gothic idea, the interior was very open and of a 'hall-church' character. The design included no separate chancel and the clergy stalls occupied a position not far from central. At the west end he planned a narthex, acting as both baptistery and porch, for his outer porch was eliminated as an economy. Double arches gave access from this low-ceilinged area into the height of the main body. Above these arches a large window with simple tracery allowed a view from the ringing chamber into the church, and permitted plenty of light from the great west window of the tower to enter the building. The roofs were unusual. The north aisle, where the large windows and gables were such a feature, employed transverse tunnel vaults, while on the south a wooden lean-to roof continued the main pitch and was supported by solid tie-beams on a coving. The nave ceiling was flat and boarded, but above each pier was a kind of fan coving over the ends of the roof timbers. It has been suggested that it was intended to paint the flat boards and that this explains the different carpentry, but no evidence of this survives. The vestry was planned for the north-east corner on two levels. The upper one was reached by an excessively steep staircase, and has a window into the church itself.

It is not recorded how Webb saw the church in use, but the great width and short distance from front to back seats permits adaptability for varying sizes of congregation. The centre area fills first, with little scope for the empty front pews of most churches. Then the sides fill up, and only when the congregation is a large one are the pews behind the choir stalls in use. Webb's plan was, of course, influenced by a very confined site, but he was essentially a practical designer, and one wonders if he planned for this adaptability.

Webb's estimate was that, without the belfry stage of the tower, it would cost £6,070. The committee raised eight queries which included whether the vestry and organ chamber could be transposed to remove the chimney from the north side; whether the position of the pulpit could be changed; and whether he intended the ringing chamber to be open to the church. His reply stated that his composition of the north side was carefully considered, and the chimney was so placed to get the best draught and also to balance the tower artistically. He explained that the mullioned screen between ringers' loft and church would be glazed.

Meanwhile the plan had been sent to Mr Du Cane, the clerk to the Earl's trustees, and he wanted to know the state of the fund and the likely additional cost of the organ, fittings and furniture. In August Forster was urging haste, so as to obtain a faculty to demolish the existing church. This was granted on 1st November, after the Bishop of Carlisle (Harvey Goodwin) had made a number of suggestions, including apparently the addition of two more dormer windows on the south side. Late that month George Howard, before leaving for Italy, wrote to Forster expressing a strong view that the committee should accept Webb's advice to postpone the building of the bell-tower for a few years.

In February 1876 Webb's surveyor was taking out the quantities and Webb had communicated with eight builders, but only two of them were prepared to tender. He tried to avoid advertising but wanted to find a 'man of good repute to undertake the work'. However, it became clear that advertisement was necessary, and even after advertisements had appeared, only three tenders were received, all of which exceeded Webb's estimate. He commented that 'building is as costly in the North as it is in the South'. There was further advertisement for tenders in October. This time Beaty Brothers, of Wetheral Quarry, were given the contract in December. By February 7th 1877 the contract was ready for sections 1 and 2 of the quantities, the sum mentioned being £5,678-6-3. Webb was keen that gas should not be used in the church as it does 'serious injury to public buildings. A few lamps or candles at the darkest season of the year would be all that would be necessary in a country parish like Brampton'. However he agreed to prepare schemes for lighting with gas and heating with hot water. He was in touch with a likely clerk-of-works, Mr J Morland, who had considerable experience of church work with Cory and Ferguson. He required to be certain, however, that he could come with Cory and Ferguson's goodwill. There was an idea of appointing another man for ten shillings less than Morland's £3, but George Howard pressed for Morland's appointment by telegraph 'having a very strong opinion on the subject of clerks of works myself, and knowing how unfortunate the results of having a bad one – as in the case of the Brampton workhouse – may be.' Morland was appointed.

The last services in the doomed church were held on 4th March 1877, the Bishop having licensed the Infant School in Moat Street for the celebration of Divine Service during the taking down of the old church and the erection of the new one. Whitehead had the school arranged every week to look as much like a church as possible. His predecessor, Miller, had met with great opposition in introducing what seemed to him a more seemly ritual. Whitehead sought similar improvements and used the school to prepare for the change so that, when services began in the new St Martin's, people were quite accustomed to the improved order. A surpliced choir, choral service, orderly ritual, free and open seats, were all accepted without antagonistic feeling.

The foundation stone was laid on 12th July 1877 but the Bishop of Carlisle could not be present as he was on holiday. The ceremony was performed by George Howard[6] as is recorded by an inscription at the west end of the north arcade. The ceremony took place at noon and was followed by a public luncheon at the Howard Arms, the tickets for which cost three shillings. It must have been a select company at that price. In a cavity under the stone was placed a bottle containing, among other things, copies of the *Carlisle Journal* and *Carlisle Patriot* and a penny of 1876 coinage.

A problem arose immediately the work began, because Mr Thomas Routledge, owner and occupier of the house to the east of the church, communicated with the vicar through his solicitor, Mr Hough, 'his apprehension that his lights may be interfered with by the building of the new church'. Forster sent a copy of the letter to Webb, commenting that he thought Routledge had no grounds for action seeing that a public street intervened between the properties. Webb conceded that there might be a very slight diminution of light, but 'as the church is a public building for the good of the town, and as we could not have used the site for the new church without placing it as we have, Mr Routledge is not likely I should think to object in any way when he knows the circumstances. For if the church had been built elsewhere that part of the site would have had to be let for building on, and cottages, small shops, or a forge or or public house would really have injured Mr Routledge's property, whereas the church will considerably enhance the value of it, and the loss of light, if any, will be so trifling that it is not worth consideration in any other way than I have mentioned above.'

Webb underestimated Routledge. The latter attended a meeting of the committee on 14th May and stated his intention to take proceedings if his lights were in any way interfered with. Forster asked Webb to come to Brampton without delay to consult with the committee, and he postponed the building of the vestry. Webb wrote instead of coming, deploring Routledge's want of public spirit, and enclosing drawings to demonstrate the degree of the loss of light. He said that if nothing could be done he would redesign the vestry to bring it down within a line of 45 degrees from the sill of Routledge's ground floor window. George Howard agreed with Webb's view. Webb came to Brampton in June and saw Routledge and Hough on Carlisle Station, where he drew diagrams to show how little he would gain by redesigning the vestry, and refused to consider the removal of the vestry to another part of the building. There was a pause in activity in the matter until the following April when Hough wrote again, claiming that it was now apparent that the access of light and air had been materially affected. They claimed compensation which they hoped could be fixed in a friendly and amicable manner. It was December, however, before Hough named the sum claimed in compensation, £150, 'although he considers that his property is damaged to a greater extent than that.' Forster consulted Webb, who still felt that Routledge had little to complain about and much to be thankful for in having a substantial public building opposite. He thought the claim of £150 surprising, as a slight alteration of the ground floor windows, at a cost of £30 or £40 each, would admit much more light than he had before the old church was pulled down. He felt that Hough's proposal of arbitration would be expensive for the parish. Routledge was prepared to reduce his claim to £100 or go to arbitration. The committee offered £50 and Routledge agreed as he was 'wishful to avoid unpleasantness and considering also the object of the building by which he is injured'. He further required that his costs of £6/6/0 be paid. The committee refused this condition and Routledge finally accepted their offer 'though feeling that he had not been fairly treated'. Mrs MA Harding who also had property affected 'owing to the wall of the new church being extended so far east' so that her tenants were complaining, made a claim for compensation, but does not seem to have pressed it.

In Webb's explanatory letter of March 1875 he had defined the purpose of some of the liturgical furniture.

> The so-called prayer desks are in reality mere extensions of the stalls westward – the desk facing west on each side is intended for lettern use (*lettern* is an archaic spelling of 'lectern') instead of a separate lettern – however these desks could be omitted and a lettern standing clear substituted. The exact position of the pulpit as shown need not be insisted upon but it would not do to put it more eastward, as that would be into the stall spaces, or behind the stalls, but it might be moved south, as then the sloping roof of the south aisle would act as a sound board, but I have myself no fear but that all persons in the church would be able to hear the preacher distinctly.

In August 1878 Mr Whitehead must have suggested that no pulpit as such should be provided, for Webb wrote, 'I think the proposition in your letter… is a very good one with regard to the pulpit'. He asked Whitehead to instruct the clerk of works to stop work, if it had begun, on the pulpit. A free-standing lectern was, however, supplied.

By September 1878 the church was ready for consecration and Whitehead asked the Bishop for a date for this. Harvey Goodwin replied that he could give one, but 'if the building is complete at the time at which it is expected and promised to be, it will be something novel in my experience'. The consecration was fixed, appropriately, for St Martin's Day, 11th November, and the Bishop preached at the service at 11.00 am.

St Martin, detail from the east window

A poster for the consecration of the church, 1878

BRAMPTON PARISH CHURCH.

THIS CHURCH WILL BE CONSECRATED

ON

Monday, November 11th,

(ST. MARTIN'S DAY),

BY THE

LORD BISHOP OF CARLISLE.

THE SERVICE WILL BEGIN AT 11 A.M.

There will be EVENING SERVICE the same day at 7-30.

A Collection will be made at each Service in aid of the Church Building Fund.

Books of the Consecration Service, 1d. each, may be had from Mr. Cheesbrough and Mr. Hodgson.

All seats in the Church are free and unappropriated.

THERE WILL BE A

PUBLIC LUNCHEON

THE SAME DAY AT THE

HOWARD ARMS HOTEL

AT 1-30 P.M. ;

Tickets for which, Five Shillings each,

may be had from the Churchwardens, or at the Hotel, not later than Friday, November 8th.

The Hon. C. W. G. HOWARD, M.P.,

WILL TAKE THE CHAIR.

H. Whitehead, *Vicar.*		T. Forster,
Brampton, October 30th, 1878	*Churchwardens.*	G. Gilmour, T. Phillips, T. C. Thompson.

Thomas Cheesbrough, Printer, Brampton.

SOME PROBLEMS

Financial problems remained. There was a deficit of several hundred pounds and the guarantors had to be called upon. The architect's fee, which was on a 5% basis, had to wait until Beaty's account was presented. His travelling expenses were divided with the Naworth estate for which he was working at the time, building a house called Four Gables for the agent, Christopher Stephenson. The Trustees offered a further £250 with the request that it should be used to pay the architect. George Howard, in paying a further £5 of his guarantee, regretted the decision to 'offer money to Mr (Thomas) Routledge the tanner' and hoped the payment for building and furnishing would take precedence 'of this extraordinary grant'. In March he wanted to know the financial situation and whether George Routledge had paid the £100 promised for the porch. He also reminded Forster of the decision to publish a subscription list. Mr JG Grey, an agent at Naworth, was called for his guarantee and paid £16/8/0. Evidently he died soon afterwards for in August 1879 his father wrote from Wooler for an explanation of the circumstances 'as he had no interest in the church excepting to oblige Mr G Howard. I think it is very hard that he was called upon to pay this'. Presumably Forster replied as there is a postcard from Millfield, Wooler, merely saying: 'Yours recd. with thanks. I wish it had been for a better cause than that precious warehouse of a place. Yours obtly, GA Grey.'

The debt remained awkward and George Howard addressed a remarkable letter to Forster on 30th August 1879, which is worth being given in full.

Naworth Castle

Dear Mr Forster,

I understand that, at the last meeting of the Brampton Church committee, it was decided that no steps should be taken for the payment of the debt on the church, as the committee thought that I had better undertake that duty, I was certainly surprised at this decision of the committee, as I believe that the committee are jointly responsible for the payment of the debt, and I cannot admit that there is any obligation on me to undertake the whole of the responsibility in this matter.

I hear that the wish of the committee that I should pay their debt, was supported by the following statements:

1   That the people of Brampton never wanted a new church, but were induced to undertake the building by one of my family.

2   That the choice of architect was owing to my advice.

3   That the committee have had no control over the alterations in the plans, which were arranged by myself and the architect.

4   That no more money is to be got out of Brampton.

I will answer these statements in order.

1   I must entirely dispute this statement, it is the exact contrary of the truth as far as my family and myself are concerned. At the time that a meeting in favour of having a new church in Brampton I remember that both my father and I were anxious not to press this matter or to urge it, unless we found that the opinion of the meeting was entirely in its favour.

2   It is true that I recommended Mr Webb. I promised to increase my subscription if the committee would employ Mr Webb; the committee accepted my offer. I cannot see that, having accepted my subscription the committee are thereby relieved from further responsibility.

3   I think that reference to the minutes of the meetings of the committee will prove this statement to be inaccurate. Without going into detail I may mention several cases of additions and alterations not suggested by myself or Mr Webb: two windows added at the suggestion of the Bishop, alterations to the choir stalls at the suggestion of Mr Whitehead and other parishioners, and the porch for which order was given by Mr Routledge, but the additional expenses which are much more important, were added by the committee against my advice; they are for the heating and warming of the church and for the organ. These changes I thought and said at the time should be met by a separate subscription and ought not to be charged to the building fund. The approximate cost of these items amounts to £490 or very nearly the total amount of the present debt. I am quite ready to share in any effort made for raising this same. I and my family have not been backward hitherto but l do not think that the fact that we have provided the larger part of the sum collected should make us responsible for the whole of the additional charges which I have named, charges which are not usually included in the cost of building a church, which do not depend on the architect or his design; but which belong to the conduct of the church service and to the comfort of the congregation, and which should in my opinion be met by the parishioners. The last printed list of subscriptions will I think justify this opinion. It shows that Lord Carlisle's trustees, family and guests have subscribed about: £3602

Other persons not residing in the parish of Brampton £1096

Anonymous subscribers £110

Church collections, interest etc. £260

The parish of Brampton £1754

4 The fourth statement that was made that no money is to be got out of Brampton may be true at the present time. As I supposed that this would be a bad time for collecting money, I proposed that amount of the debt should be borrowed, so that time might be given for some attempt to raise money. I understand that the people of Alston raised £542 towards the expenses of their church in 1870 by a bazaar and again £567 in 1874, besides other sums raised by work, tea meetings etc. Surely the cost of the organ might be met by a bazaar at Brampton? For I must repeat that I consider that this debt is due to the organ and fittings and can not legitimately be considered a building debt. If the committee will undertake to provide for the expense of the organ which is I believe £250 – by a bazaar or otherwise; I will on my part engage to pay the architect and the remainder of the debt, which will be £250 more – considering this as a donation for the lighting and warming of the church, I had intended to make a proposal of this kind before I heard of the decision of the committee. I have been obliged to protest against the statements which I understand were made at the last committee meeting and to explain that I do not consider myself solely responsible in this matter and that my present offer is purely spontaneous. I hope the committee will now agree with me so that the difficulty in which we are placed may be removed by our joint efforts.

I shall be much obliged if you will communicate my letter to the committee.

Yours truly,

George Howard

It seems clear that there was some resentment at the very close association between the architect and Mr Howard, and a feeling that he had taken too much upon himself. Whether the committee's decision was a 'try-on' to see how much responsibility he would take for the debt we cannot tell, though they may have felt that his distinction between building and other costs was somewhat subtle. However, one cannot but admire the tact and politeness of the letter, allowing a face-saving get-out to all, and a prompt payment of fees to his friend Webb. His letter nevertheless received no immediate reply and he wrote again on 7th September, complaining that a meeting had been held for which he had not received notice.

Another problem arose in connection with the organ. From a letter by Webb dated 13th July 1878 it seems that an old organ was being purchased and he had visited Kentish Town to see it. A Mr Robson was working on it and having considerable trouble through rot. Two years later it was in position but suffering from damp. Thomas Richardson, a churchwarden, wrote to Webb about this and he replied:

> … I would say that organs always suffer considerably on being placed in new churches; and, considering the thickness and solidity of the walls of your church, it is quite certain that it will be several years before they are dry. I see no reason whatever to doubt of the building becoming in time thoroughly dry; for, happily, the foundations are on good dry sand and rock, but the particular construction used to make the church a dry one would be apt to make its drying matter of some time. For instance, the damp-proof course applied to keep moisture from rising in the walls, also hinders the water used in their construction from uninterrupted descent into the ground, consequently the walls have to dry wholly from the surfaces… I would urge on the churchwardens the necessity of taking particular care to air the building in every possible way. During all fine days from sunrising to sun setting the doors should be kept open.'

He urges ventilation at great length and also the slow and long use of the heating apparatus and the examination of rain-water heads and pipes for stoppage. Problems continued, however, and in September 1883 Whitehead inquired about decay in the patent wood block floor. Webb referred him to Mr Thomas Gregory of Station Works, Clapham Junction, the manufacturer, and was rather at a loss to explain the reason. In April 1884 he carried out an inspection and reported that the wood block floor was in a 'singular state of decay', sending samples to a chemist for analysis. He was convinced the cause was wet rot and that water was finding its way under the church and being drawn up by the warmth of the heating apparatus, the increase of heat because of the use of the building and the gas lighting, through the compact sand and concrete. Some slates were decaying on the south aisle; the gabled roofs over the north aisle had shrunk through timber shrinkage; there was settlement in the tracery of the circular window and over the main door. His recommendations included the following:

> The laying of a drain along the south side to carry off water; each block of seats in turn to be removed, the wood flooring removed, the ground taken out to the necessary depth, brick sleeper walls built to carry the oak sills of the pews and a boarded floor provided with sufficient ventilation; under the choir stalls the blocks to be removed, the concrete painted with stockholm tar, and the blocks replaced; the good wood blocks to be used at the west end of the south aisle, where there are no seats; the outside area of the east window to be opened out and fitted with Lazonby flags; slates of the wrong kind which had been included on the south aisle to be replaced by best Westmorland; removal of lead and renewing of timber work over the north aisle; the wedging up of the arch of the main door and the joints run with lead.

Webb suggested that the work be done by the Naworth estate clerk of works and men. He felt some responsibility for the defects to the north aisle, and for his own satisfaction, offered to meet the cost of this work. He later sent to Mr Stephenson, the agent of the estate, a cheque for £25 to cover this, saying that he was sending it to him rather than to the churchwardens, as the latter would probably ask why it was not £100, and would think him a fool for doing such a thing voluntarily. The cheque was later returned to him, presumably on the instructions of George Howard. This incident illustrates vividly the 'Arts and Crafts' morality which Webb exemplified. Webb never undertook enough work to become wealthy and the sum involved here must have been a significant one to him.

In August 1885 Webb wrote to Stephenson to complain that the gas lighting which had been installed against his advice 'regardless of the character of the building, has annoyed me'. He spoke of the well-considered scheme of decoration and claimed that the newly-devised plan of gas lighting was a mistake, fatal to his scheme; that it would certainly be injurious to the stonework and walls, and 'is in character too childish for a serious building'. He could not believe that Mr Howard had anything to do with it, and declared that if application should be made to him at a future time as the designer of the building for advice on any matter in connection with the church 'I shall be obliged to refuse to have any more to do with it whatever.' He excluded Christopher Stephenson from this condemnation, for from him, he said, he had received nothing but courteous treatment. This is not untypical of Webb's treatment of clients. He expected to be consulted about everything and trusted entirely, saying to any who demurred, 'there are plenty of other architects'. Fortunately he seems to have forgotten his threat eighteen years later when he was asked about the completion of the tower.

Webb thoughtfully provided the churchwardens with a set of drawings for future use and these are among the valued records of the church, but he seems to have remembered his work in Brampton with little pleasure. In 1902 he wrote to William Weir at the Society for the Protection of Ancient Buildings:

> I had never seen any representation of the building since I left it to the clumsy carelessness of somewhat unliftable citizens of a really mean north country town. I can assure you that when I handed over the work to them some 25 (or so?) years ago they were by no means anxious to express any pleasure in the result of my work.

BUILDING THE TOWER

Because the committee could not see its way to meeting the full cost of Webb's design, it had been decided to build only the base of the tower and give it a temporary pitched roof just high enough to hold the bells. The original impressive design of a tower with octagon and spire, as shown in Webb's drawings, was never completed, and it was nearly thirty years before the tower was finished at all. Seven years after Whitehead's death in 1896, his widow offered £500 if the work were undertaken in her husband's memory. The vicar, Thomas Armstrong, wrote to Lord Carlisle (the former George Howard) asking for a 'substantial contribution as patron' towards the tower's completion. There is a draft of a letter in Lord Carlisle's hand stating that he could not comply, as a sufficient contribution had been made to the building of the church, which is a 'unique example of art which is already an object of interest and admiration to the rising school of architecture'. He insisted that the architect for the completion should be one who was in full sympathy with Webb's work. This letter was probably never sent, for only three days later, on 18th February 1903, he wrote promising to confer on the subject on his return to Cumberland. In April Mr Cheesebrough wrote on behalf of the parish to ask Lord Carlisle if Webb was still living as they wished to have his views. Two Carlisle architects, Martindale and George Armstrong, had already been approached before this, but Charles Ferguson, as advisory architect to the Diocesan Society, had advised that 'it would be a sad misfortune if so admirable a design as Mr Philip Webb's for completion of the tower should not be carried out'. Ferguson was clearly 'in full sympathy' with Webb's work, for it was he who, in the meantime, had designed St Martin's Hall next door in a style which misled Nikolaus Pevsner into attributing it to Webb.

Lord Carlisle confirmed that Webb was indeed alive, though living in retirement and poor health at Worth in Sussex. He offered a contribution, which eventually came to £600, conditional upon Webb's design being used. Webb wrote to Lord Carlisle from Caxtons at Worth on 2nd October, saying that he had searched his papers and found three studies for the top of the tower. 'I concluded', he wrote, 'after the body of the church was finished that the upper part of the tower would have to be considerably simplified, not only for improved effect (which at that time I could well consider) but in a less costly way. Later on, and merely for my own satisfaction, I made two or three studies for the completion, should it be carried out in my lifetime.' He left the choice of architect to Lord Carlisle and the parish, not wishing him to be 'tramelled by my instructions unless he was personally familiar with myself and my work.' He suggested that George Jack should act as sole architect in consultation with himself. He gave Jack a strong recommendation, mentioning that he had been his assistant for many years, had completed Mrs Morris's cottages at Kelmscott and was highly thought of by WR Lethaby. Jack was indeed a disciple, who held Webb in the greatest reverence, and collected his sayings. Born in the United States, he was Morris and Co's furniture designer and designed needlework, while his wife worked as an embroiderer. Webb suggested that Jack should prepare measured drawings and supervise the work, being paid as architect in the usual way. 'In no case would I accept any payment for putting the matter clearly before him.'

A year later Webb wrote, 'I do not care if the committee completed Brampton Church Tower from a design by an architect chosen by themselves but I could not agree to any architect not chosen by me using any design made by me (and particularly the small scale drawings showing the then supposed finish of the tower) for I would much prefer such architect should be free to make something he considered fitting, than that he should make a jumble of anything of my doing'.

It was decided to take Webb's advice and to entrust the work to Jack, using one of Webb's sketches. Jack visited Webb at Worth, and found him 'working steadily, although naturally slowly on account of his infirmities, at the details of drawings of masonry'. Webb seems to have designed all the details, though a beautiful drawing in the possession of the church is signed 'George Jack, Superintending Architect'. Jack had some difficulty in acting as go-between. His proposal to appoint his nephew as Clerk of Works was rejected, and a member of the committee, Mr A Routledge, undertook the work at a salary of thirty shillings a week. Jack stood out for walls four feet thick in certain portions, reducing to three feet six in others and decided to use hard-burned local brick for the bands inside the tower.

Webb would have liked to employ the builder who had built the church, Beaty of Wetheral Quarry, but finding that he was dead, four Carlisle builders, James Beaty,

Beaty Brothers, J and R Bell and John Laing and Son were invited to tender. They were to take out their own quantities. The tenders varied between £2,060 and £1,644/10/0. The lowest, Laing's, was accepted. Jack's fee for drawings, specifications etc was 2½% of the estimated cost and 2½% for the remainder of the work including supervision. Webb refused any payment. It was decided to provide a clock at the same time and John Smith of Derby quoted £108 plus £11 for each of the two additional dials. It would require winding twice a week. Laing's estimate included: mason and bricklayer £1258, joiner £235, plumber £151/5/0. Johnstone and Roys, the joiners, were to provide scaffolding for the spire from the height at which the builder's work ceased. The time stipulated was until the end of 1905 with a penalty for exceeding that time at £5 a week. Work began on May 16th and before long Jack reported that it was proceeding satisfactorily though not as fast as the builder had contemplated, 'but I never believed he could do it in the time allowed, nor did I at any time wish the work done at such a rate of progress as he proposed. It would be harmful to hasten the building of such thick walls which require time to adjust themselves if a firm piece of building is to be expected.' He was full of praise for Routledge's work.

On 12th September the vicar and Colonel Riddell appeared before the Chancellor of the diocese in his consistory court and were granted a faculty for the building of the tower. The legal costs amounted to £5/15/0.

Problems arose. The stone was to be from Gelt Quarries, but it was found that the amount of stone suited to the very high quality external work required was only one eighth of that quarried. Laings normally expected that half would be suitable for outside and half for inside use, but Gelt Quarries gave a stone of rather poor quality. To obtain stone from Cove Quarries would cost 9d per cube foot plus 6d carriage by rail, as against the price of 6d and 2d carriage for Gelt stone. Cove Quarries seem to have been in Scotland in the Lockerbie area. Mr Laing junior (later Sir John Laing) attended the meeting of the committee to explain the problem, saying that the extra cost would amount to £35. The committee offered £25 and Laing said he was sorry to hear of their decision. Even the £35 would not fully cover the change and he assured them that 'the largest subscribers to St Martin's Church tower would be Messrs John Laing and Son.' The committee decided to refer to Mr Jack the question of increasing their offer to £30, but £25 was the sum finally paid.

In Roy Coad's biography[7] the builder's reminiscence is quoted:

> As there was one type of stone repeated several times, before we made up the tender, I got one of our masons to dress a stone like that and see how long it took him. I told him that he must not work extra hard because I was going to base a tender on it, but he must have been either more skilful than the average, or he had worked more industriously, because I lost £100 on that job.

Another problem concerned belfry louvre boards. Jack found that Webb's improved design for these would cost £11/14/6 more than estimated. He conceded that extras were vexatious, but claimed that no architect can wholly foresee his design in detail, as the design develops, and if possible improvements should be accepted. The committee rejected the new design and Jack wrote again asking them to reconsider their decision. He can 'foresee that there will be great trouble ahead of us… Mr Webb is quite fixed upon this and says he is going to write to Lord Carlisle upon the subject, and as Lord Carlisle has the most entire faith in Mr Webb's judgement in architectural matters, he will no doubt feel that his wishes should be carried out'. He argues the matter at some length, urging not to 'spoil the ship for a ha'porth of tar', that 'it would break the old man's heart to have his best effort, probably his last in this direction, flung back upon him because his client wished to be economical as he thinks at the wrong time'. Lord Carlisle's subscription was on the understanding that Webb's judgement should be final. 'Now please let us have your sanction to spend this miserable dozen pounds and so make an end of what I can well see will embroil us all round and be a very bad beginning to the life of your tower − what is it after all − a few pounds and as you are so much in debt, it won't make so much difference to be just a little more. Time is going on and if I don't hear soon that your committee agree to my proposal, I expect the Church Tower will be opened without louvres'. On another occasion Jack spoke of Webb as 'a very particular man indeed' and one can hardly envy him his position as intermediary. The committee 'after much thought and consideration resolved that uninfluenced by any considerations in your letter the Committee under protest sanction the new design for the louvre windows. The committee also resent the threat that if your proposal was not carried out the tower be opened without louvre windows, which they consider was entirely uncalled for.' Webb had always been very determined with clients. In spite of his

Socialism, he, like Morris, found himself always 'ministering to the swinish luxury of the rich', but he found it easier to deal with rich men of taste than with a small town committee, whose economical attitudes seemed to him cheeseparing.

At last the work was done, and the tower dedicated on 10th May 1906 by Bishop Diggle of Carlisle. The account came to £1,706/18/3, and Jack's fee to £84/1/0. His travelling expenses from London for seven visits were £16/12/0 and his hotel expenses paid to Mr Riddell £4/19/0, 'which was considered very satisfactory'. The committee also had the pleasure of receiving from Mr Jack a long and interesting review of the new tower. Besides Mrs Whitehead's £500, Lord Carlisle had given £600 and the rest had been raised by subscription. So all seemed happy at last. Webb's great work was completed before his death, the tower could rise nobly above the Brampton roofs, Mr Whitehead was suitably commemorated, and the generosity of Mrs Whitehead and Lord Carlisle, of Brampton parishioners – and even of John Laing and Son – had made it all possible.

The dedication ceremony was marked by speeches. Canon Rawnsley sent an apology and as was his habit appended a verse.[8]

Mrs Whitehead spoke to the company in St Martin's Hall afterwards, mentioning her husband's resolute refusal to hold bazaars (though *bona fide* sales of work were different), and Lord Carlisle also spoke. He started rather ambiguously with the words:

> There is only one thing which I regret very much in the proceedings today and that is that the Bishop was not a personal friend of Mr Whitehead, because I feel that had he been he would have been able to tell you something that would have been of value.

He spoke about Webb:

> I confess that when this church was originally built I was a strong partisan of Philip Webb and perhaps prejudiced in his favour; but a good deal of water has run under the bridge since that time, and I feel that I can look at his work more critically than I perhaps could do then. I should admit perhaps that there are faults here and there… but time… has shown his real greatness. He was one of a small knot of people, all of whose work is represented in this church, and who have really changed the whole current of decoration and

architecture in England. The school that is now universal in the country are imitators, consciously or unconsciously, of Webb and Morris. If you go out of London on the railway you see whole colonies of little houses that are built in the spirit and in imitation of Philip Webb; and this school of building… gives a character to modern English architecture which makes it very much better than you can see in Germany or France… It was owing to Mr Whitehead that the church as it stands is such a perfect example of that school. It was owing to him that Mr Webb's church was given windows by his friends and co-workers Morris and Burne-Jones. The consequence of that is that in Brampton you have a unique monument which will become more and more striking as years go by.

That same year (1906) Mrs Whitehead decided to commemorate her husband further by placing a terra cotta relief of Saint Martin dividing his cloak with a beggar by the main door. She brought back from Venice a photograph of a panel of a door in the Ducal Palace and commissioned a Miss Rope to execute the work.[9] JH Martindale designed a moulded frame for it. Lord Carlisle told Jack about it, and Jack replied that it would probably be all right for 'Miss Rope is a good workwoman and I am pleased she got the thing to do. I have not seen Mr Webb… and I don't think I shall mention the matter to him. I don't see that it can do any good, and he might feel that he should have been consulted.' Jack knew Webb. Mrs Whitehead suggested that some inscription might be placed upon the sill, but this was not done. 'Some day no one will know anything about it', she wrote and had it not been for the survival of her letters among the Howard papers, they would probably not have done so. She felt proud that it was the work of a woman artist.

Back in 1882 a curtain had been provided behind the altar. On 10th January Morris wrote to George Howard:

> We had a letter from the parson's wife of Brampton asking for patterns for the same. I bid them send a big worsted pattern which I thought would be best, as 'tis mostly blue, which I fancy the Church wants; only you must think that under that very bright window all woven stuffs will look gray. If the blue looks grey, I fear there is nothing for it but the brightest red; we have a woollen stuff very bright and telling (3 ply pomegranate), or would red damask silk be too costly?

No record seems to exist of what was chosen, but a Morris curtain was provided under a gesso relief panel of corn and grapes, probably the work of Kate Faulkner.

In 1907 the then vicar was suggesting that a new reredos should be provided, so replacing the Morris curtain. Lord Carlisle wrote saying that it is 'desirable to be excessively careful as to design. At present, the church is as far as I know, unique as a specimen of the work of Webb, Morris and Burne-Jones, because there is no detail or accessory that is incongruous. If you were to put in a permanent piece of woodwork (however good the design might be in the abstract) that was not in harmony with the other work, it would be an eyesore and would diminish the value of the rest. If you think it essential to replace the curtain (which I had thought good) you had better ask Mr Jack who would consult Mr Webb and would at all events give a design in the same character as the rest of the work.'

Nothing was done about a reredos until the 1920s, when the Morris curtain disappeared.

The reverence for the unity of conception and design, which Lord Carlisle so emphasised has remained a tradition in the parish, and nothing has been done to upset this unity. As early as 1891 it was decided, under the incumbency of Samuel Falle, to tile the sanctuary. Webb was consulted and he recommended 'a dullish red marble in preference to the ordinary flooring tiles'. The estimated cost was £45 and it took several years to raise this, but the work was completed in 1894. In the 1920s it was suggested that an 'English altar' with curtains and posts surmounted by figures of angels might replace the older furnishings, but the Diocesan Advisory Committee showed a similar respect for the unity of design and rejected this proposal. In its place another design by Hicks and Charlewood was substituted, which incorporates the Morris gesso panel of corn and grapes which formerly surmounted the curtain.

Two items of furniture, added after the building of the church, are of interest. The font cover in memory of Mrs Whitehead, was the work of the Keswick School of Industrial Art, under the direction of Whitehead's friend and biographer, Canon Hardwicke Rawnsley. The school was one of the many results of Morris and Webb's Arts and Crafts philosophy. The enormous umbrella stand, intended for a position under the west window, was designed and made by a local craftsman, using motifs designed by Webb for the clergy stalls.

THE BRAMPTON WINDOWS

It is easy to imagine that George Howard must have hoped, when the church which had been designed by his friend Webb was completed, that the commissions for stained glass windows would go to the Morris firm, with which he was so closely associated. But this was not, like some Victorian churches, built by the wealth of one family, where the provision of stained glass was seen as part of the project. Although the Naworth estate had found about half of the cost of the building, it was only when a memorial was needed that they contributed directly to the glass. There seems to be no evidence as to who suggested the policy regarding the stained glass, but it is clear that it had to wait for donors prepared to use it as a memorial. It is on record, however, that the committee decided that no mural tablets would be permitted in the main body of the church and that windows would be the acceptable form of memorial. Whether this was because of any dislike of mural tablets, or because of a determination to direct finance into obtaining windows, we do not know. Tablets from the old church found a place in the narthex and in the south-west corner.

On April 24th 1877, long before the building was completed, Webb wrote a letter to Forster, which seems to imply that a proposal had been made about glass. He writes:

> I am naturally much interested in the proposal, as it will altogether depend on the character of the stained glass put into the window as to whether the church will be injured in appearance or not. Messrs Morris, of 26 Queen Square, Bloomsbury, do all such work for me, and I do not know any other stained glass manufacturer on whom I could depend for work in accordance with the design of the church and of sufficient artistic excellence.

Six months later he again wrote to Forster, enclosing an estimate from Morris and Co for glazing three windows on the north side.

> When I last was at the church, I stated that it would be best to consider any part of the ornamental glazing of the windows with regard to the whole; therefore, the accompanying note is arranged in accordance with that resolution… From Messrs Morris's estimate you will see that the cost of these three windows, framed according to my directions on a system appropriate to

the character of the building, is at a lower rate than when I was talking with you on the subject I told you was probable, so that it has seemed to me as likely that your subscription would enable you to put in two of the windows and the third would be supplied by the gentleman who proposed to glaze one as a memorial to a member of his family. I have examined the designs for the figures and find them noble pieces of work, and very satisfactory to me from the art point of view. The cost of packing and fixing would probably amount to £7 or £8 each window if fixed separately, if the whole were fixed at one time the cost would probably be no more than £20.

Among the surviving correspondence there is no indication that subject matter was discussed or proposals made from the parishioners' or donors' end. Yet the whole scheme as completed bears witness to a non-doctrinal, liberal Christianity, with a total absence of representations of the great moments in salvation history, or the great doctrinal themes. This might, of course, fit in with Whitehead's Broad Churchmanship and Howard's Unitarianism, but we can only conjecture. The scheme described in Morris's estimate was finally completed with only two modifications. Webb's hope, however, that the first three windows could be immediately commissioned did not materialise.

The remainder of this chapter deals with the windows in the order of their installation. They are however numbered in clockwise order beginning in the northwest corner.

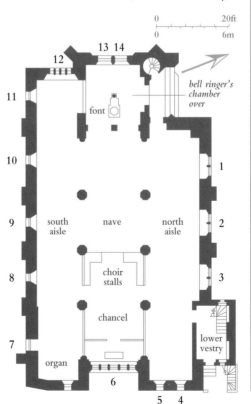

The Fall, Adam and Eve
detail from the tracery light
Window 1

FIRST LIGHT ~ *WINDOW 1*

The window commemorates Joseph Coulthard who had died seven years before the window was made in 1878. It seems to have gone ahead without further discussion Coulthard was the first headmaster of Brampton National School and later the founder of a private school called Croft House Academy. He seems to have been a remarkable teacher, totally opposed to the use of corporal punishment and fines in imposing discipline. He was active in good works, including managing the Savings Bank.

This window, like the two which followed it, consists of four large figures with a background of floral quarries and one small tracery light. Top left is Adam, in white, holding a spade and described as *Homo Primus*, the first man. The design had been made for the nave south window of Jesus College Chapel, Cambridge in 1874.

Below is Enoch (or *Enos*, for Latin titles are used). He is in blue, dark blue and green, with a book in his right hand, while his left hand holds another hand which reaches down from Heaven. Genesis 5: 24 tells us that Enoch walked with God. He is described as 'Patriarch'. The design was made for the west window of Calcutta Cathedral which Morris supplied in about 1874. It was in memory of the Viceroy, Lord Minto, who died in 1872.

The top right figure is Noah (*Noe* in Latin). He is in green and dark red and holds the ark in his left hand. The dove brings a branch over his left shoulder. He is described as '*Predicator*', or preacher.

Below is Abraham in yellow and gold over silver armour, holding a long sword and with a helmet. This would seem to refer to the battle in Genesis 14: 14-16. The design was first used at Frankby in the Wirral, where he is described as 'heir of the world', a quotation from Romans 4: 13.

The little tracery light is of *Adam and Eve* to a design made for Lamerton, Devon in 1877. That church was destroyed by fire in the same year and the only other use of the design was in a tracery light at Albany, New York, made in 1881.

FOUR FOGIES ~ *WINDOW 2*

One of the leading laymen in the church building project was William Carrick, a solicitor and partner with Mr Lee in the firm which acted for the Naworth Estate. He died before the completion of the church and his son decided to commemorate him by giving the second window. Things do not seem to have run smoothly, for Webb's draft letter dated 16th March 1879 runs as follows:

I have delayed answering your letter of the 5th until I had seen Messrs Morris and consulted with them in the matter of your window. The practice of sending out designs for stained glass windows from which donors may select that which most pleases them, is only followed by the regular manufacturers of stained glass in the gross – It would not be done by artistic workmen, such as Messrs Morris, who have to pay very highly for their designs. Also, in fitting to windows appropriate glass, all the circumstances of the case must be taken into consideration – two of the most important being, the character of the architecture of the building in which the glass is to be placed, and the system on which all the windows of the building are proposed to be glazed. In the designs sent for glazing two of the three windows on the north side of the nave, Messrs Morris have closely followed my explanations as to what character of glass would best fit the position, and I beg to say that I was much pleased with the drawings forwarded which were arranged direct from the full sized cartoons made by the artist. It is quite possible that you would be better pleased with a design applicable to a window in another position of the church. Messrs Morris say that they have cartoons which would do for the three light window on the south side of the south aisle of the chancel arranged in this way (drawing) namely three single figures in the upper part of the lights and subject panels at the bottom of lights. But this window would most likely cost more than the window on the north side.

The square windows in the south aisle of the nave and the west window (circular) of south aisle would require artist's designs to be specially made for them, and therefore would relatively be more costly. If you should decide upon abandoning the design sent to you for one of the north aisle windows Messrs Morris would have to charge you £2/10/0 for the use of the drawing, the drawing itself being still their property.

Moses
Window 2

Allow me to say in conclusion that, as the designer of the church, I am very anxious to have stained glass in its windows of the best character and fitted for the building, and I particularly wish to avoid the use of harsh crude designs and inharmonious colouring, the ugliness of which spoil most of the churches in which they are placed.

The letter seems to have achieved its object, for the 'solicitor and coroner for East Cumberland' is commemorated in a window as originally proposed. The top left figure is Moses in dark red holding the tables of the Law, described as *dux* – commander. He has horns, as often in ecclesiastical art. This is based on a mistranslation of Exodus 34: 29-35 in the Vulgate or Latin Bible. Moses' face 'shone' as a result of being in God's presence, but the word is an unusual one and St Jerome translated it as 'horned', and artists followed that idea. The design was made in 1866 for Glasgow Townhead Blochairn Church. Below is Solomon in gold with a crown and a model of the temple in his hands. This design was made for the Calcutta Cathedral west window. Top right is David, described, like Solomon, as *rex* – king. He is in green and white, and playing a harp. This is again from a design for the Glasgow Townhead window, against which Burne-Jones enters in his account book '4 fogies. Moses & Co. £7 each £28.

'The lower right figure is Elijah the prophet in white and deep red, hands raised, being fed by a raven (1 Kings 17: 6). This is another Calcutta design. The tracery light has an inscription – *O Gloriosa quod Heva tristis abstulit tu reddis almo germine*. In a letter from Morris's dated 17th October 1878 reporting the sending of the second window, comes the rather curious explanation for the inscription taking the place of the proposed 'demi-angel playing some musical instrument'. The verses chosen refer to the tracery lights in the other two windows, of the fall of man and the Annunciation of the Virgin. They may be translated:

> O glorious maid
> That which was lost to hapless Eve
> Thy holy scion did retrieve.

'Without this explanation the allusion would be obscure,' the letter says. One might have thought that the linking of the Fall with the announcement of Salvation made sense without the obscurity of the Latin poem! The poem itself is from a sixth century hymn to the Virgin Mary by Venantius Fortunatus.

The third window hung fire. A Mr Scarf of Birmingham wished to erect a marble monument in memory of his wife, and Forster asked him to consider providing a window, as the first two in memory of Mr Coulthard and Mr Carrick were much admired. Scarf claimed not to believe in stained glass, but Forster reported that the committee had resolved 'that no monuments or tablets be placed in the body of the church', and offered Scarf the choice of a tablet in the porch or a third window. Scarf replied tersely 'the committee having announced their decision the matter is at an end. I cannot beautify Brampton Church or paint its windows.'

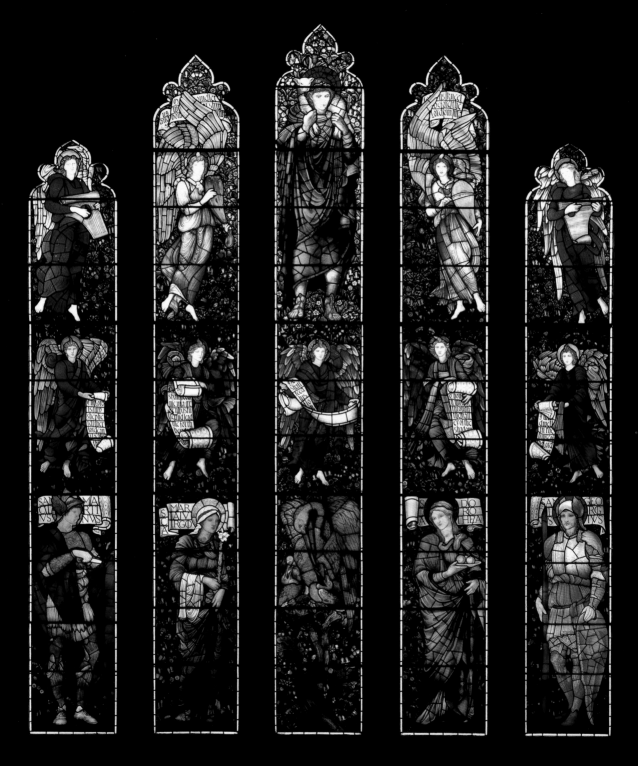

A MASTERPIECE OF STYLE ~ *WINDOW 6*

Carrick's death was soon followed by that of the chairman of the committee, Charles Howard. He was much loved in the district, which he had served as member of Parliament for many years. The decision to commemorate him by providing an east window appeared in the press, and letters were received from two firms, Wailes and Strang of Newcastle, and Powell Bros of Leeds, offering to make the window. It was, of course, a foregone conclusion that Morris would provide this window in memory of George Howard's father, and Burne-Jones made special designs for it. As soon as Webb heard of the plan he sent a donation of ten guineas mentioning his 'strong and loving admiration for the dignified and kind-hearted old man'. On 6th June 1879 Morris's submitted an estimate for five large figures and nine small ones (angels) and a tree background for £667 excluding packing and fixing. On 27th August 1880 Morris wrote to George Howard describing the window:

> There are three rows of figures, the upper part has in it the figure of Christ as the good Shepherd surrounded by floating angels carrying scrolls inscribed with verses from the 23rd Psalm, the figure of Christ is robed mostly in purple; the angels are coloured in various shades of red and blue.

> The lower part of the centre light is filled with a 'Pelican in her piety' *ie* the bird tearing her breast to feed her young; this legend from the bestiaries having made the pelican one of the types of Christ. On the south side of this symbol stands first St Dorothy clad in purple and blue and next St George in red golden armour; on the north side are first the Virgin Mary clad all varying shades of blue and next St Martin in the act of dividing his cloak with the beggar, his armour is coppery in hue, and his cloak crimson. The whole background of the window is a diaper of flowers of the deepest colours and much broken mosaic-fashion.

Apparently Burne-Jones's share of the price of the window was £200 as the May 1880 entry in his account book reveals:

> To Brampton window – a colossal work of fifteen subjects – a masterpiece of style, a *chef d'oeuvre* of invention, a *capo d'opera* of conception – fifteen compartments – a Herculean labour hastily estimated in a moment of generous friendship for £200, if the firm regards as binding a contract made

The east window
Window 6

from a noble impulse, and in a mercenary spirit declines to re-open the question, it must remain – but it will remain equally a monument of art and ingratitude – £200.

Lady Burne-Jones in her Memoirs of her husband, says that such an entry would be written quickly with a grave face, and the book immediately closed and put away.

All the designs in this window were designed for it, but some of them were much repeated subsequently. The figures of St George and St Martin were the most used of all Burne-Jones stained glass designs. Sewter records their use 44 and 40 times respectively. The others were little repeated and the Pelican not at all. The cartoon for this was later coloured, and was given by Sir Frank Brangwyn to the William Morris Gallery at Walthamstow. The cartoons of the Good Shepherd, St George and all the angels are in the Carlisle City Art Gallery, Tullie House. Sewter records that the St Martin was in America in 1970. The cartoons of The Virgin Mary and of St Dorothy were sold at Sotheby's around about 1980.

The choice of the four figures in the lower part might seem a little curious until one realises that St Martin was the patron saint of the parish church from very early times, and Mary, Dorothy and George were all Howard family names.

The Pelican design is one of Burne-Jones's most remarkable. He took a standard piece of iconography mentioned in the quoted Morris letter, but set the nest on a twisted tree. This has been seen as a departure point for Art Nouveau, and the cartoon is used in Pevsner's *Pioneers of Modern Design* to illustrate this.

Sewter comments that the angels seem full of movement when one looks at them separately, yet they counterbalance one another so exactly that the effect of the window as a whole is one of timeless stillness.

Morris wrote to George Howard: 'I am very glad indeed that you think the east window a success; I was very nervous about it, as the cartoons were so good that I should have been quite upset if I had not done them something like justice.'

Charles Howard was also commemorated in Lanercost Priory, again with a Burne-Jones design. The mural tablet includes profile heads of Charles and Mary his wife, and metal plaques of the Nativity and the Entombment, the work of Sir Edgar Boehm. The plaques are to designs by Burne-Jones.

The Pelican in her Piety,
from the east window
and the cartoon by
Burne-Jones, with later
colouring

POSTERITY WILL APPROVE ~ *WINDOW 3*

This window did not have to wait long. Alexander Thom MRCS, a local medical practitioner, died in January 1880. Whitehead preached his funeral sermon and remarked later to Peter Burn, 'My sermon did not please everybody. I said too much for a man irregular in his attendance at church. You and I knew the man, Mr Burn, and we saw in him what others failed to see. The people have yet to learn that Christianity is not in observance but in life.' This quotation from Peter Burn[10] goes with another which gives important information about the Brampton glass.

> Though of a passive nature, he could, when the case demanded it, manifest a master-spirit. This he did at a committee meeting convened to consider the question of placing a window in St Martin's Church, to the memory of the late Dr Thom. Some were for buying at the cheapest market; but he argued that harmony of design should be sought rather than the saving of money. They had already a window executed by Messrs Morris, the design of the poet artist Burne-Jones, and, as vicar, he would rule that the work be entrusted to Messrs Morris. He was sorry to cross his friends, but he acted for posterity. The time would come when the people of Brampton would approve of his action. Shortly before his death he said to me, alluding to that meeting, 'I have never regretted my step, Mr Burn; I still hold the opinion I then expressed; Posterity will approve of the action. Believe me, the time will come when strangers will seek Brampton, not for the sake of the town itself, but for the windows in St Martin's Church, the work of the honoured and world-famed Burne-Jones.'

The window itself followed the original scheme, except that St Luke replaced St John Baptist, probably because it was now a memorial to a doctor. The two top figures are of the evangelists, John and Luke. The original use of these was at Jesus College, Cambridge, where each of the four evangelists is set between two of the classical Sibyls. Burne-Jones received £15 for each figure. Both are striking designs each with its attendant symbol, the eagle for John and the winged ox for Luke, and each holding the book of his gospel. John is in blue, while Luke, who rests his foot on a stump, is in green and pink. The St Luke design is also to be seen at Lanercost Priory in a window erected four years earlier. The other two figures are of St Peter and St Paul. The first was designed for the hall of

Peterhouse, Cambridge, and holds a key (Matthew 16:19). Here he is in green and brown. St Paul's design was made for the same Glasgow window as those of Moses and David – two more 'fogies'. He is in blue over red, with a book and a sword. These attributes are found from at least the 11th century; the sword refers both to the instrument of his reputed martyrdom and also the 'sword of the spirit which is the Word of God' the Christian's weapon in fighting the good fight (Ephesians 6:17). The Peterhouse commission is the subject of another amusing entry in Burne-Jones's account book.

> September 1871. St Hugh, St Peter, St George… £36. Slight and hurried in handling I admit – but there is my own vigour of design and massive treatment of drapery. Now I am off for Italy with the money I have so honorably earned.

Burne-Jones had written £45 but this has been deleted and on the opposite page is a note – 'I am very sorry, but the words of the tariff are 'up to 4ft £12, over 4ft £15'. Burne-Jones has added 'I also am sorry and very much more than you. EBJ.'

The two little windows in the north east corner, now the chapel, were left, but otherwise the provision of stained glass was proceeding more or less in a clock-wise order.

CHARITY, AT £7 ~ *WINDOW 7*

Only four years later Mr Carrick's partner in the law firm, Mr John Lee, died. His wife Mary had died ten years earlier. Their children undertook to provide glass for this window. The design adopted, as has been mentioned earlier, was first used at Christ Church Oxford. Faith and Hope appear in Burne-Jones's account book for January 1871 at £15 each. For some reason Charity in the previous month is given as £7, with the note:

> Charity (not exercised by the Firm – therefore keep the cartoon and hang it up) £7. *NB* My liberality in the matter of the cartoon of Charity – (charged £7) demands a special account – £7 for a colossal cartoon of four figures – and this in the 14th year of my professional life – what irony is involved in the title of this cartoon – Charity!!!'

Female figures representing the Cardinal Virtues occupy a light each, with 'the greatest of these' in the centre. A singularly beautiful set of drawings, they were much used by the firm. Apart from the use of individual examples, eight windows of the set were made before the end of the century. They show a remarkable diversity of treatment. The Oxford window has a background of dense foliage and fruit; the Harrow Weald one has a limestone wall with daisies and other flowers growing between the stones; the Rochdale one has a flowering hedge, and shows the virtues trampling on their opposite vices, Despair, Envy and Folly. Here in Brampton the backgrounds are patterned but in deep colours, against which the robes of the figures stand out each in its own distinct colour, blue, pink and red. Hope is on tip-toe, stretching upwards towards heaven, Faith holds a tiny flame and about her feet a serpent is coiled, while Charity is tranquil, holding in one hand a larger flame and in the other a baby, while other children cling to her. The window returns to a typical Philip Webb arrangement of Morris's early years, with a band of colour set between bands of clear but flowered quarries. The Firm now had a catalogue of designs, showing the glass painters employed on each window. *Faith* and *Hope* were by Bowman, *Charity* by Dearle, and the quarries and scrolls by Stokes.

Rather unusually the discussion about the subject of this window has survived in family papers belonging to a direct descendant of the dedicatees. The idea of an original Burne-Jones design was given up for reasons of cost and the family took a great liking to the Oxford *Three Virtues* design. However Morris said it had been done several times and he did not want to repeat it; but Mr Lee was so keen he enlisted George Howard's support and Morris agreed to it. He must have provided the background.

Faith, Charity and Hope
Window 7

TRAGEDY AND LOSS ~ *WINDOWS 8, 9 & 10*

The sad fact is that if windows are financed as memorials, they inevitably wait on tragedy and loss. The three small windows in the south aisle represent the most tragic story of them all. George and Rosalind Howard had eleven children, and although five died before the age of 38, only one died in infancy. This was Elizabeth or Bessie, the tenth child, who died on 15th April 1883. She had been baptized at St Martin's and was only four months old. She was buried in the ruins of Lanercost Priory and a beautiful effigy was erected there, the work of Sir Edgar Boehm. Her parents commissioned Morris and Co to make three windows with scenes of childhood in the New Testament. They are arranged with the outer windows having two roughly square panels surrounded by quarries. The designs for these had been made in 1876 for Paisley Abbey and Burne-Jones received

Elizabeth and John

Salome, with James and John

£6 for each. In the Paisley window the four are predella panels each beneath an appropriate figure – Salome, the Virgin Mary, St John Baptist and Eunice. Here they are given more individual treatment. The Paisley window, at the time of writing, is rather dirty and the little subjects are hardly noticeable, but here they form some of the loveliest of Morris and Co's small windows. They have no texts, so it seems worth recording the texts shown in Latin at Paisley. On the left is Elizabeth with the child John Baptist. 'Many of the children of Israel shall he turn to the Lord' (Luke 1:16). Below is Salome with her children, James and John. 'One at thy right hand and one at thy left in thy kingdom' (Matthew 20:21) a curiously unsuitable text, as this was their request which, they were told, it was not the Lord's to grant. In the right hand window above is Eunice and the child Timothy. 'The Lord give you understanding in all things' (2 Timothy 2:7). This panel suffered serious damage by vandalism in 1977 but was most skilfully restored by LC Evetts.

Christ blessing children

Below is described as *Holy Family*, with Mary seated and Jesus and John at her knee. The text is 'Let the children of Zion be joyful in their King' (Psalm 149:2).

The fifth subject, that of the central window, was specially designed by Burne-Jones and represents Christ blessing children. It was Burne-Jones's third design of this subject and was only subsequently used once, at Monifieth near Dundee. In his account book it is entered under November 1887 'a design of Christ blessing little children for Naworth – £15'. The catalogue of designs records that the easternmost window was painted by Dearle, and the others by Bowman, the quarries and scroll etc by Pozzi and Stokes.

THE CHILDREN'S WINDOW ~ *WINDOW 11*

This was designated the Children's Window and the cost of £34 was raised by offerings made at the baptism of children. It is dated 1897 and is similar in character to the previous three. The panel is of Samuel saying to Eli, 'Here I am for you called me' (1 Samuel 3:5). Oddly enough although the inscription tells us that it was erected by the children of Brampton, the text is in Latin. This may be because the design was made for a window in Christ Church Cathedral in Oxford. The Oxford window was made to commemorate an undergraduate, Frederick Vyner, who, while on holiday in Greece, was captured by brigands and

died in their hands. His mother erected the lavish church of Christ the Consoler, Skelton, on the family's Newby Hall estate in Yorkshire and also the Christ Church window in his memory. The latter has four of the outstanding 'young men' of the Bible, Samuel, David, John the Evangelist and Timothy, with predella panels beneath of incidents from their stories. For each of these latter designs Burne-Jones received £12/10/0.

Samuel and Eli
Window 11

WELL DONE, THOU GOOD AND FAITHFUL SERVANT
~ *WINDOW 12*

In 1896 Henry Whitehead, who had been the originator of the new church, died. In time the tower was to be completed in his memory, but only ten days after the funeral a public meeting was held to consider a memorial. Officials were elected including Peter Burn as treasurer, and subscriptions were solicited. Samuel Falle recorded in the parish magazine that it was proposed to fill the round window in the south-west corner with glass to a Burne-Jones design and to erect a tombstone. Unfortunately the whole matter degenerated into controversy over a proposal to found a scholarship instead. The Countess of Carlisle offered £200 which she promptly withdrew, claiming that some person (never identified) had stipulated that the scholarship could only be tenable at a 'Church School'. Mrs Whitehead then said she would provide the window, and soon afterwards the vicar reported that enough money had been received to fill the four lights of the west window of the narthex with Morris glass representing four acts of mercy. A design was made for the round window, a lightly drawn pencil drawing of which is in the William Morris Gallery at Walthamstow. It is of a Last Judgement, or perhaps it would be more accurate to call it a Day of Resurrection, for all appear to be rising heavenward. Christ occupies the top light and in each of the others there are two or three figures rising. Why a change was made is unknown – perhaps in the interest of economy, for the final design was made up from three previous ones. The window itself is very unusual. It is more or less round with a tracery head consisting of an irregular decafoil with two small rhomboidal apertures, the lower part divided by two mullions. In the decafoil is the *Reception of souls into Paradise*. This was designed for Calcutta Cathedral in 1874 and Burne-Jones received £20 each for this and other subjects, but it does not appear in the Calcutta window as described by Sewter. The two angels in the outer lights with long trumpets almost like alpenhorns were designed for the remarkable window at Cheddleton, Staffordshire. That window made in 1869 is unique in being coloured almost entirely with silver stain. There are three angels in the Cheddleton window which is of orthodox shape. Here the centre angel is omitted and the design of the others is adapted by cutting off the bottom corners. This sounds rather drastic but has been successfully achieved. Burne-Jones received £10 for each angel. The centre lights are of figures adopted from a window in the

Illustrations of this window are shown inside the cover

Wren Church at Ingestre, Staffordshire, in memory of the Countess of Shrewsbury. On the 1890 Ingestre window the scrolls bear the words of Christ and Mary at the cross in Latin. Here they are replaced with 'Well done, thou good and faithful servant, enter thou into the joy of thy Lord' (Matthew 25:23). These last windows employ a different method of creating flesh tones, giving more transparency. Peter Cormack remarks on this change: It seems that, from some period in the late 1880s/early 1890s Morris and Co started using a pink potmetal for flesh areas in some of their windows as opposed to their former practice of painting flesh-coloured enamel on the white glass for faces, hands, feet etc. The latter technique, because of the somewhat unreliable firing of the flesh enamel, has led to the deterioration in some of the flesh parts of the east window. The flesh-pink pot metal is obviously not subject to this kind of decay, but it lacks the potential for subtle moulding that one has by using enamel. The painters of this window were Campfield, Stokes, Bowman, Walters and Dearle. It was the last window on which Campfield worked.

FOUR MAJOR PROPHETS ON A MINOR SCALE
~ *WINDOWS 13 & 14*

Although these windows and window 12 were proposed at the same time to commemorate Whitehead, these were completed earlier. But here too there was a change of plan, and the acts of mercy gave place to four prophets. These four figures were designed for a window at Tavistock in 1875, which also contained the four Jesus College evangelists and the *St Paul*, also repeated at Brampton. Burne-Jones's account book entry for 1875 recorded: 'Tavistock, 4 Major Prophets on a minor scale designed I regret to say with the minimum of ability £5 each £20.' By 1898 Morris was dead and supervision would be by Dearle. Veal, Bowman, Walters, Titcomb and Wren all had a hand in the painting. One cannot but feel there is a falling off from the quality of the earlier windows.

There the great enterprise reached its conclusion after twenty-one years, but the two little windows in the north-east corner remained without stained glass.

St Michael
slaying the Dragon
Window 5

SACRIFICE AND VICTORY: A POSTSCRIPT
~ *WINDOWS 4 & 5*

After another twenty-two years the memorial to the fallen of World War I provided an opportunity to rectify the omission. The north-east corner was refurnished as the 'Soldiers' Chapel' and two little Morris windows provided on the subjects of *Sacrifice* and *Victory*. Sewter does not record the designers, merely the subjects of *Christ carrying the cross* and *St Michael and the Dragon*, and that the painters were Glasby, for the figures, and Watson, for the quarries, scrolls, borders and inscriptions. Dearle made the design of *Christ bearing the cross* for Rottingdean in 1919 which is here named *Sacrifice*. His *St George* for Rottingdean was subsequently given wings and became *St Michael Slaying the Dragon* for Fochabers and then at Brampton. The late Don Green worked this out and wrote, 'One can speculate that the Scots may not have been too keen on any suggestion that victory in the Great War had been largely due to the patron saint of England; whereas St Michael was perfectly acceptable as a champion.

PROTECTING THE GLASS

The protection of the glass is a matter of urgency today, because of an increase in vandalism. However this is no new manifestation. In October 1878 when the first Brampton windows were ordered, Webb wrote:

> Messrs Morris avoid putting wire guards on their windows wherever the place in which they are fixed is quiet and orderly. I do not know sufficient of Brampton to be able to speak of its general civilization. But I should think Mr Whitehead would be able to educate his boys up to the point of appreciation of the beauty and value of the pictured glass. Any of the boys showing a turn for drawing might be set to studying and copying the figures, and thus a respect for the very beautiful glass would be engendered. If the place is very rough and the boys unteachable wire guards must be put up but they are very injurious to the effect of the glass.

Whitehead does not seem to have been very confident regarding the civilization of the town or of his educational capacities, for wire guards were put up. By the 1970s they had rusted away and some vandalism had taken place, the damage being repaired by LC Evetts. In 1976 the east window was protected with a double glazing of 5mm Oroglas G sheets held between double hardwood battens. This cost £821, which was raised through a Stained Glass Festival. The remaining windows received new galvanised mesh guards at a cost of £640.

Protecting Angels,
detail from the east window

The Annunciation,
detail from the tracery light
Window 3

THE STAINED GLASS OF MORRIS
& HIS FRIENDS

As we have seen, Burne-Jones was involved in stained glass design from the age of 24 and when the firm began in 1861 stained glass soon entered its repertoire. There was at the time an enormous demand for stained glass, as the ideas of the Oxford Movement, with its glorification of the Mediaeval church, spread. In 1861 a number of substantial firms were in existence: Williment; Wailes; Warrington; O'Connor; Ward and Hughes; Powells of Whitefriars; Lavers and Barraud; Heaton, Butler and Bayne; Hardman; Gibbs; and Clayton and Bell. Their inspiration was the work of Augustus Welby Pugin in recovering a mediaeval art, and their work was usually imitative of that art. The new firm's intention, in spite of the members' love of the mediaeval, was to bring the work of modern artists into this active craft. Morris wrote to his former tutor, the Revd FB Guy, asking for a list of clergymen to whom it might be of any use to send a circular. He said, 'You see, we are, or consider ourselves to be, the only really artistic firm of the kind, the others being glass painters in point of fact (like Clayton and Bell) or else that curious nondescript mixture of clerical tailor and decorator that flourishes in Southampton Street, Strand.'

At 8 Red Lion Square they rented premises in which they installed a kiln, and appointed George Campfield as foreman. Morris had come across him as a pupil at evening classes at the Working Men's College and he is said to have been employed by Heaton, Butler and Bayne. Among early employees, were boys from the Boys' Home in Euston Road, run by a Colonel Gillum, one of the firm's early patrons.

It was the architect, George Bodley, who gave the Firm its first opening. Starting on his own independent career, he was designing a small church for Selsley, Gloucestershire, and commissioned a complete set of windows. Very soon more orders followed for his churches at St Martin's Scarborough, St Michael's Brighton, All Saints and Cambridge.

For these churches designs were produced by Burne-Jones, Morris, Rossetti, Ford Madox Brown, Webb, Marshall and probably Campfield and others.

Webb produced the whole window designs, in which a band of coloured subjects was set between bands of plain quarries (like the *Faith, Hope and Charity* window at Brampton). This idea was drawn apparently from mediaeval glass in the chapel of Merton College, Oxford. Morris himself designed the colour schemes and lead patterns, and supervised the whole. About these early windows there is a certain naivety, which lasted only a short time. By 1865-6 with examples like the east windows of Middleton Cheney and Catton they had produced some of their finest work. Webb's bands of quarries gradually disappeared, but still there was no attempt at three-dimensional pictorialism. All is on the flat plane of the glass with figures and groups now often placed against wonderfully varied and imaginative backgrounds, which must have been very much the contribution of Morris, whose genius for pattern expressed itself in this way – foliage, clouds and occasionally stars against a dark blue background.

At this stage quite a lot of secular commissions were undertaken, like the Harden Grange windows based on the story of *Tristram and Isoude* (now in the Bradford City Art Gallery), the *St George and the Dragon* panels (in the Victoria and Albert Museum and repeated at Cragside), and the *Good Women, Poets and Scholars* in the Hall and Combination Room at Peterhouse, Cambridge. Rossetti made a considerable contribution here.

Gradually, however, the operation changed. In 1874 Morris decided that, as most of the original partners were taking little part in its work, it was right to convert it into a company of his own direction. This provoked resentment by Madox Brown, Rossetti and Marshall and there was a good deal of unpleasantness before the firm became Morris and Co. Webb and Burne-Jones were happy to waive any claims and to continue to design for the Firm, but from this time onwards Burne-Jones was virtually the sole designer of cartoons for stained glass. But Morris's other activities were giving him less time for supervision, and some of the glass painters like Dearle were given more responsibility. A further change was that Burne-Jones's designs were becoming more pictorial, sometimes being spread across mullions. By the 1880s there are signs of decline, which continued after Morris's death, though the firm continued to produce worthy glass into the 1930s. It is with the large set of windows at All Hallows, Allerton, Liverpool, that the change becomes apparent. Brampton, while contemporary with Allerton, shows little sign of this move to pictorialism. The east window, specially designed by Burne-Jones in memory of Charles Howard, keeps to great figures arranged on a flat plane, but against a remarkable floral background, and with probably the firm's most daring use of colour.

The quantity of the stained glass of the Firm is surprising, and generally quite unknown until Sewter's researches. At a rough estimation some 500 windows were produced before the death of Morris, and well over 1000 in all. They are to be found all over England, Scotland and Wales, as well as in the USA and countries of the British Commonwealth. Within reach of Brampton they can be seen at Lanercost, Kirkbampton, Haltwhistle, Ponsonby, Irton, Armathwaite, Plumpton and Cliburn.

One interesting aspect of their work is its absence from Cathedrals. Only Oxford, Peterborough and Salisbury of the older cathedrals have examples, but there are windows in the churches at Birmingham, Blackburn and Bradford, which later became cathedrals. The reason for their absence elsewhere is Morris's antagonism towards the 'restoration' of ancient buildings, expressed in SPAB. He refused to make a window for Westminster Abbey and in about 1881 a circular was issued stating that 'We are prepared as heretofor to give estimates for windows in churches and other buildings, *except in the case of such as can be considered monuments of Ancient Art*, the glazing of which we cannot conscientiously undertake, as doing so would seem to sanction the disastrous practice of so called Restoration'. An interesting case was that of St Philip's, Birmingham, which became the cathedral in 1905. Dating from 1715, it is a fine baroque church by Thomas Archer and was the church in which Burne-Jones was baptised. Such a building did not apparently come within Morris's definition of 'Ancient Art', and between 1885 and 1897 four impressive windows of great size and representing one subject each without interrupting mullions, were placed in the church.

There was a tariff of prices to be paid to members of the firm for first use of their cartoons, fixed in 1871. This included those over four feet high – £15, two feet six inches to four feet – £12, one foot eight inches to two feet six inches – £10. This was later varied a certain amount. When cartoons were reused a further royalty of ten per cent was paid. We have already seen that this caused Burne-Jones some chagrin, as it was so much less than he would have received for his paintings. The re-use of cartoons, a practice employed by other firms, enabled prices to be kept down, and did not at all signify a lesser quality in the window concerned. The overall design, the colour scheme, the background and the lead design was worked out individually for each window. An interesting example is the set of Faith, Hope and Charity figures, designed by Burne-Jones for Christ Church, Oxford in 1871 (BJ 147, 148 and 149). They were used in all some thirty times, either together or separately. A comparison of the Brampton window with the Oxford one, which is remarkably different, can hardly fail to credit the re-use with greater merit.

Some Morris windows have deteriorated and much of the detail has been lost. One example is in the charming east window at Kirkbampton. Morris and Co were not alone in suffering this deterioration; it affected many makers in the 1870s. The explanation is found in a letter of Morris to George Howard written in 1880:

> We (and I believe all other glass painters) were beguiled by an untrustworthy colour, having borax in it, some years ago, and the windows painted with this are going all over the country. Of course we have taken warning and our work will now be all right. We have given instructions to our men to take out the faulty glass, which we will – restore! – at once and pay for that same ourselves – worst luck. Borax is the name of the culprit: the colour makers, finding that the glasspainters wanted a colour that would burn well at a lowish temperature, mixed borax with it to that end; but unluckily glass of borax is soluble in water, and hence the tears wept by our windows – and our purses.

By the time the Brampton windows were made the fault had been corrected.

In 1883 Ruskin apparently inquired from Morris about the techniques involved in making their windows. In reply Morris wrote:

> … *We* paint *glass; first the lines of draperies, features and the like, with an opaque colour, which when the glass is held up to the light is simply so much obscurity; with thinner washes and scumbles of the same colour we shade objects as much as we deem necessary, but always using this shading to explain form and not as shadow proper.*

2nd Finding that it was difficult to get a flesh-coloured glass with tone enough for the flesh of figures, we use thin washes of a reddish enamel colour to stain white glass for flesh colour and sometimes though rarely, for other pale orange tints: NB. this part of our practice is the only point in which we differ from that of the mediaeval glass painters.

3rd We use a yellow stain on white glass (or on blue to make greens): this is chiefly done by means of silver, is quite transparent and forms part of the glass after firing; it may therefore be considered rather a diffusion of the colour in the glass than a painting on it.

The body of the glass is of two kinds, first what is technically called pot-metal, in which the colouring matter is fused with the glass and essentially part of it: and 2nd what is called flashed glass, in which the white body is covered with a coloured skin: this is done by the workman taking on the end of his hollow rod first a large lump of white metal, then a small dip of coloured metal; he then trundles the lot, making a disc like a small piece of crown glass. This kind of glass however is not much used except for red coloured by copper called technically 'ruby', this owing to its make is often curiously and beautifully striped and waved: this glass is, I must tell you, perilous to fire the painted colours upon, as the kiln generally changes it more or less, sometimes darkening it almost to blackness, sometimes carrying the colour away: to avoid this risk we are sometimes obliged to paint the necessary lines on a piece of thin white glass and lead up the two together; this, which is called plating, I have sometimes done with two pieces of coloured glass, to get some peculiar tint: one must be careful not to overdo the process, however, or you will get a piece of glass at once cumbrous and liable to accident.

I should mention that all the glass is very thick: and that in some of the pot-metals, notably the blues, the difference between one part of a sheet and another is very great. This variety is very useful to us in getting a jewel-like quality which is the chief charm of painted glass − when we can get it. You will understand that we rely almost entirely for our colour on the actual colour of the glass; and the more the design will enable us to break up the pieces and the more mosaiclike it is, the better we like it…

Stained glass is never cheap, and Morris glass was more expensive than that of some contemporary firms. The Brampton windows give an idea of price.

The small 'Children's Window' cost £34, the three tall north ones an average of £117 each and the great east window £667. Webb pointed out that if it was necessary for artists' designs to be specially made, the window would be relatively more costly.

The firm soon moved from Red Lion Square to 26 Queen Square, Bloomsbury. In 1877 a showroom and offices were opened in 449 Oxford Street and in 1881 the Merton Abbey works became the studios and workshops.

Morris died in 1896 and Burne-Jones two years later. The firm continued with little reduction in its business, but the real power had gone. JH Dearle became the chief designer. He was a very able imitator of Morris but his work has no originality. Burne-Jones cartoons continued to be used and when the first World War created a great demand for 'heroic' memorial subjects, his *St Martin* and *St George* designed for Brampton, came in for frequent use. They appeared in such windows at least a dozen times. On Dearle's death WH Knight became chief designer but in 1940 the firm closed down.

Angel, east window, cartoon by Burne-Jones

FIVE REMARKABLE VICTORIANS

In the account of the building of Saint Martin's, a number of interesting personalities appeared. It seems worth recording some details of the principal ones. The idea of the new church was that of the vicar who came to Brampton in 1874, Henry Whitehead. The support of George Howard, the future 9th Earl of Carlisle, was vital and it was he who pressed for the appointment of Philip Webb as architect. Webb's was the controlling conception in the creation of a most unusual piece of architecture. When it was finished, its principal feature became the set of stained glass windows, placed in it between 1879 and 1896 by Morris and Co, William Morris's firm, to the design of Sir Edward Burne-Jones.

HENRY WHITEHEAD *(1825-1896)*

Besides his notable work in Cumberland, Whitehead has the extraordinary distinction of being the person who proved that cholera was communicated through drinking water.

Born in Ramsgate and educated at Lincoln College, Oxford, he was ordained and served curacies in London. In 1859 he was curate of St Luke's, Berwick Street, Soho, when a disastrous cholera epidemic occurred, which was particularly severe in that neighbourhood. Such epidemics swept across Asia and Europe and arrived in Britain at frequent intervals after the first recorded outbreak in 1831. The cause was unknown, but two theories were put forward. The first was physical contact or contagion and the second was 'miasma'. The latter idea was that in heaps of refuse, marshy land and stagnant water, there lay a dormant disease, which could be liberated by an unknown agent, perhaps temperature, barometric pressure or lightning. The virulence of the disease was terrifying and, as both sets of theorists advocated cleanliness, Edwin Chadwick's great sanitary campaigns were made possible by fear of cholera.

The 1859 outbreak in Soho was sudden, and within ten days 700 people died in a circuit of 250 yards radius. Whitehead was active in trying to help the sufferers but it was after the crisis was over that he made his main contribution. John Snow had a medical practice in this largely slum area and, while practising in Northumberland, had already formed a third theory, that whatever it was that caused the disease was carried in drinking water. During the outbreak he prevailed upon the local authorities to remove the handle of the Broad Street pump, which lay at the centre of the outbreak. Whitehead was not convinced and set out on an exhaustive inquiry in the area involved. It took him three months and 'slowly and reluctantly' he came to the conclusion that Snow's theory was proved and he also managed to discover how the well had come to be polluted. It was a dozen years before Snow's theory, and Whitehead's proof of it, was generally accepted and another thirteen years before the micro-organism responsible was identified.

Meanwhile Whitehead had become a notable Broad Church vicar of St John's, Limehouse and in 1874, at George Howard's invitation, he moved north to Cumberland, where he spent the rest of his life. His fourteen years in Brampton were notable for the building of the new St Martin's, a healing of the divisions caused by Miller's reforming zeal, a close friendship with non-conformists like Peter Burn and an enthusiastic study of local history. As a Broad Churchman he dissociated himself from the bitter disputes over burial rights, which poisoned Church and Chapel relations. He had a strong interest in education and carried out another survey like his London one, to find out how desirable it was to have a further school in the parish. He supported the conversion of the National or Church School into a Board School after the passing of the 1870 act and became its chairman. He committed himself to the task of achieving a set of Morris windows at St Martin's.

After leaving Brampton, he had short incumbencies at Newlands, near Keswick and at Newton Reigny and from 1890 to his death in 1896 he was vicar of Lanercost. The completion of the tower, three of the windows and the sculptured relief of St Martin were all provided in his memory. He was buried at Brampton Old Church and a cross raised as a memorial there. He lectured and wrote on various aspects of the history of the district, and some of his lectures were published in the transactions of the Cumberland and Westmorland Antiquarian and Archaeological Society. The recording of church plate was a special interest and his work on the plate of Brampton deanery led to the publication by RS

Ferguson of *Old Church Plate in the diocese of Carlisle*, 1882, to which Whitehead contributed the sections on Maryport and Penrith Deaneries, as well as Brampton. He made a similar inventory of church bells in the diocese and, after his death, a set of lectures and articles was published under the title of *Talks about Brampton in the Olden Times*, Selkirk 1907.[11]

Self-portrait,
San Remo
1875

GEORGE HOWARD
9TH EARL OF CARLISLE (1843-1911)

Although his wife, Rosalind, was the subject of two biographies, one by her daughter Dorothy, Lady Henley, and one by her son-in-law, Charles Roberts, no biography appeared of George Howard. Yet in many ways he was every bit as interesting as she and remarkably different. Her interests were in politics, feminism, temperance reform and estate management, his in art. She was combative and dominating, he gentle and conciliatory. She was a radical liberal, he, though an MP for some years, took comparatively little interest in politics and became a member of the Liberal Unionists. It is not surprising that in their later years they lived virtually separate lives.

On the death, unmarried, of the 7th Earl, the heir was insane, and the estate was put into trusteeship, principally of the Duke of Devonshire. Younger brothers of the 7th and 8th Earls were Admiral Lord Lanerton who lived at Castle Howard, and Charles, later the chairman of the St Martin's Building Committee. Charles married Mary Parke, daughter of Lord Wensleydale. She was a talented painter, trained by De Witt. She died in childbirth a year later and Charles never re-married. George followed his mother's interest and after Eton and Cambridge studied at the South Kensington School of Art and later under Giovanni Costa and Alphonse Legros. He became a prolific painter in both watercolour and oils. His paintings were never offered for sale and most remained within the family. Many are landscapes of Italy, Egypt and India, besides local and other British subjects. Exhibitions of his work have been held in Carlisle on several occasions and in 1954 also in London. Bill Waters, an authority on the Pre-Raphaelites, organised an exhibition on *George Howard and his Circle* in 1968, and another on

The Etruscan School in 1978. This school consisted of British and Italian painters working in Rome between 1870 and 1900 under the leadership of Costa. Charles Roberts's *The Radical Countess* has several colour plates and many reproductions of drawings, and numbers of his drawings of Morris and Burne-Jones survive. In later life he produced an attractive Song Book, each having a whole page watercolour. This was intended as a gift to three of his grandchildren, but it was printed and copies given to members of the family, friends and associates.[12] Both a friend and patron of the Pre-Raphaelites, Rossetti, Morris and Burne-Jones, as well as Webb, he commissioned Webb to build his London house, 1 Palace Green, Kensington, which was completed in 1869 and Morris and Burne-Jones decorated the interior.

While still under 21 he met Rosalind Stanley, one of the formidable children of Baron Stanley of Alderley. In one of her letters she tells how at Christ Church Cathedral Oxford 'in June 1863, George and I on the first day of our meeting first liked one another so well that as we stood looking at the painted window which tells the life of St Frydeswyde, we knew already that each liked the other.' The window was one of Burne-Jones's earliest designs, made for Powells before the Morris firm was started. They were married at Nether Alderley Church in Cheshire, when one of her kinsfolk, Arthur Stanley, Dean of Westminster, officiated. Their honeymoon was at Naworth and there they soon settled, having a deep love of the district. In fact George was the first Earl of Carlisle for two centuries to make Naworth more than a place to visit occasionally. They had eleven children, all but one of whom grew to maturity. Their circle of friendship included many distinguished Victorians, most of whom visited Naworth: Browning, George Eliot, Jowett, Tennyson, Trollope, Matthew Arnold and Gladstone, besides their artistic friends. He succeeded to the title in 1889. George and Rosalind agreed in objecting to the rule of primogeniture. As early as 1864, in their marriage settlement, the capital of both husband and wife was assigned to trustees with the provision that after the death of both, the capital was to go in equal shares to their children, or as the surviving parent might appoint. When George died his eldest son received the entailed estate of Naworth and other properties in the area, while Lady Carlisle received the remainder of the estate for life with discretion to distribute it on her death among their children.[13] So in time the estate was broken up among their surviving children. Geoffrey received Castle

Howard; Mary, who married the Greek scholar, Gilbert Murray, received properties in the Brampton and Hallbankgate area; Cecilia, who married Charles Roberts, had properties near Brampton; and Dorothy, who married Lord Henley, property at Scaleby and Askerton.

George, whose personal religion seems to have been Unitarian, nevertheless took a great interest in the building of St Martin's. George and Rosalind were buried in Lanercost Priory.

PHILIP WEBB *(1831-1915)*

Webb was the architect of the Pre-Raphaelite circle and, with Morris, a founder of the Arts and Crafts movement. As he never employed a team of assistants and was uncompromising with his clients, his output was small. In spite of this, and the fact that he would never publish his work, he was very influential and holds an important place in architectural history. In *Pioneers of Modern Design* Nikolaus Pevsner remarks:

> Of the Domestic Revival as the movement in English town and country architecture between 1860 and 1900 is often called, Webb remained the strongest and soundest, if not the most brilliant exponent.

The son of a doctor with artistic interests, Webb wrote, 'I was born and bred in Oxford and had no other teacher in art than the impressive objects of the old buildings there, the effect of which on my natural bent has never left me.' At the age of 18 he was apprenticed to John Billing, a Reading architect, and then worked for a short time in Wolverhampton, which he hated. However, in 1852 he was able to return to Oxford as assistant to George Edmund Street, the church architect, who also designed the Law Courts in London. He was joined in that office in 1856 by William Morris who became his 'life-long friend and companion'. In 1859 he designed the Red House at Bexleyheath for the newly-married Morris, and left Street's office to work independently. He had come to see that Street's 'modern mediaevalism was an open contradiction. He resolved to try to make the buildings of our own day pleasant without pretences of style.[14]

The Red House was a landmark in architectural history, though drawing on earlier experiments in brick houses by Butterfield.

Pevsner[15] writes:

> It was built in a spirit contrary to that of the past century…Webb applied certain Gothic details such as pointed arches and high-pitched roofs; he also adopted the irregularity of the fourteenth and fifteenth-century domestic and especially monastic architecture, but he never copied. He even admitted the sash-windows of William and Mary and Queen Anne without ever being afraid of clashes between the various styles to which he went for inspiration. Red House as a whole is a building of surprisingly independent character, solid and spacious looking and yet not in the least pretentious.

In 1868 Webb designed George Howard's 1 Palace Green, Kensington, which Pevsner describes as the town architecture counterpart of Red House. Both of these survive, but much of Webb's work has been lost. Outstanding among Webb's houses which remain is Standen, near East Grinstead. Built in 1891, this now belongs to the National Trust. Brampton has two of his smaller country houses, both built for the Naworth estate. These are Four Gables, built for the estate agent, and Green Lane House, built for Whitehead.

Webb was one of the original partners in Messrs Morris, Marshall, Faulkner and Co and in the early days of the firm designed the lay-out of their stained glass windows, often using bands of quarries with a band of coloured stained glass subjects between them, so making the windows seem part of the structure. He designed the lettering and many details, especially of animals, at which he excelled. He told Jack, 'To draw animals you must sympathize with them; you must know what it feels like to be an animal.'[16]

Webb never married and always lived a life of simplicity. In later days he became a Socialist with Morris and carried his principles so far as not to invest his savings against old age. As he lived long, his later years were in near poverty, but his attitude to money was always extraordinary. When the original 'Firm' was wound up in 1875 there appears in his account book (not in his writing) – 'Arrears of Salary £640' and on the opposite side 'Claim for Salary renounced'. We have seen how, when he discovered certain defects in St Martin's, he sent a cheque for £25 to cover the cost of the repair. When it was returned he sent it again saying, 'I would not be easy at all', though Howard's determination won in the end. Moreover, when he provided the drawing for the completion of the tower and proposed that Jack should superintend the work and be paid as architect, he insisted that he would accept no payment. John Betjeman, at a meeting of the Architectural Association in 1955, described Webb as 'an ardent atheist', but the evidence seems to be lacking. Indeed it is hard to see how a man of such strong principles could have undertaken the church commission if he was. What he did include in some points for discussion was:

> If you choose to give a name to men's opinions and label me an 'agnostic' I shall not be put out, neither should I be if you called me a 'Hag's broomstick.[17]

What stands out clearly is Webb's fierce integrity. 'Honesty' was for him the key word both of his art and of his morality.

He shared with Morris his socialism, his arts and crafts philosophy and also his care for ancient buildings. Together they founded the Society for the Protection of Ancient Buildings in April 1877 and Neil Jackson has pointed out that this coincided with the planning of St Martin's. In an article in the *Architectural Review* in August 1977 entitled *A Church for SPAB* he suggested that St Martin's epitomises the reverse of the restoration philosophy which SPAB was founded to oppose.

It is impossible to read Lethaby's book without feeling the greatest respect for the character of the man. Lethaby asked May Morris for memories of him and her three pages bring out his kindliness, his love of children and animals and the music of Mozart.[18]

She talks of 'that look on his face that isn't a smile but a 'state of smiling beneath the skin'.

WILLIAM MORRIS *(1834-1896)*

Asa Briggs asks:

How are we to regard William Morris? As a brilliant designer who wasted time dabbling in other subjects? As first and foremost a poet? As a political thinker? Or as a successful blend of all these – the last 'universal man in the Renaissance tradition?'[19]

Photograph by
Frederick Hollyer
1886

Held in high esteem in his lifetime as a poet, Morris has since gained an even higher reputation as one of the greatest of the Victorians, both artist and prophet. WB Yeats saw this at the time of his death, when he wrote:

> In the literal sense of the word and in the only high sense, he was a prophet; and it was his vision of that perfect life, which the world is always trying… to bring forth, that awakened every activity of his laborious life – his revival of mediaeval tapestry and stained glass, his archaic printing, his dreams of Sigurd and of Gudrun and of Guinevere, his essays on the unloveliness of our life and art, his preaching in parks and at the corners of streets, his praise of revolutions, his marchings at the heads of crowds, and his fierce anger against most things that we delight to honour…

Born into a wealthy family at Walthamstow, he went up to Oxford intending to be ordained. There he met Edward Burne-Jones and together they turned to art. The great influences upon them were Rossetti and Ruskin, and Rossetti taught them to paint. But Morris, in spite of some lovely designs for stained glass, realised that painting was not his real talent. Where it lay emerged from the experience of furnishing and decorating the Red House with the aid of his friends. As the only one of their circle with much money, he largely financed the beginnings of the Morris firm, but it was his directive genius which extended into all its areas of work. As a pattern-designer he was supreme, and in textiles, wallpapers, tapestry, and the design of the colour, leadwork and lay-out of stained glass, he found his artistic role. To begin with he thought it might be architecture, but after less than a year in Street's office, where he met the real architect, Philip Webb, he worked at painting for a couple of years. In Oxford again, with Rossetti and others to decorate the Oxford Union, he met his future wife, Jane Burden ['Janey'], the daughter of a groom. Her striking looks came to exemplify the Pre-Raphaelite ideal of womanhood. They were married in 1859 at St Michael's Church, Oxford, when the service was conducted by another Oxford friend and poet, Richard Dixon, who in later life was vicar of Hayton, near Brampton. Already Webb had produced the designs for the Red House, which was built for them at Bexleyheath, and there they had five happy years. From the experience of decorating and furnishing the house with the help of his friends grew the idea of 'a manufactory of all things necessary for the decoration of a house', Messrs Morris, Marshall, Faulkner and Company. Pevsner claims that 'this event marks the beginning of a new era in Western Art'.[20] The firm described itself as 'Fine Art Workmen in Painting, Carving, Furniture and the metals', but in time some of its more characteristic products were embroidery, dyeing of textiles, weaving of tapestry and carpets, stained glass and wallpapers. Of Morris's work in textiles Linda Parry has written:

> William Morris comes to mind instantly as the single most important figure in British textile production… As a designer and manufacturer he was unique both in the context of Victorian traditions and the wider study of textile history. A patternmaker of genius, he explored techniques in order to get the best from his designs in colour, composition and texture. He revived long forgotten techniques of dyeing, printing and weaving, and in his own workshops, revitalized mediaeval traditions of the designer-craftsman.[21]

Meanwhile, however, Morris's reputation was established as a poet. Of surprising fluency, most of his poetry has a nostalgic quality which makes little appeal today but it was highly popular at the time and he was regularly described as 'the author of *The Earthly Paradise*.'

His marriage, after a few happy years, began to fail. Janey suffered almost permanent invalidism and it is plain that deeply as he loved her, she could make little response. Rossetti came to idolize her and to paint her obsessively. He and Morris took a joint tenancy of the lovely Thamesside Cotswold manor, Kelmscott, where she and Rossetti spent much time together. However she and their two daughters took a lively interest in the work of the Firm and in Morris's political work. Jenny developed epilepsy, giving them much anxiety, but May later took a leading part in the firm's embroidery work. Morris seems to have been determined that his wife should feel no guilt. 'Janey be happy', he wrote.

As if poetry and the work of the Firm was not enough, Morris in middle life developed four further enthusiasms.

The first was Iceland, to which he paid two visits, and the language of which he learned so that he could translate the Sagas.

The second was the protection of ancient buildings, which at that time frequently suffered extremely drastic restoration. He was the main spirit behind the formation of the Society for the Protection of Ancient Buildings in 1877 and continued to take an active part in its campaigns.

The third was the discovery of Marxism, which confirmed many of his instinctive beliefs. He threw himself into the political struggle with remarkable dedication, with public speaking, writing and generous financial support. His *News from Nowhere* is an idyllic account of a post-revolutionary society where 'commercialism and profit-mongering' was a thing of the past. There was always a tension between his craft work, which was inevitably costly and his conviction that 'I do not want art for a few, any more than education for a few, or freedom for a few…'. He once turned on Sir Lowthian Bell with the words, 'I spend my life ministering to the swinish luxury of the rich'.

The fourth interest, which came very late, was printing. Influenced by Emery Walker's researches into old books and manuscripts, he resolved to design his own type and in 1891 established the Kelmscott Press. In this Burne-Jones, who was out of sympathy with his political activity, was a valued supporter, supplying beautiful designs for woodcut illustrations. The press produced some of the most lovely printed books ever made and it had a good influence on the development of printing design.

In 1896 the amazing energy flagged and he died at the age of 62. He was buried at Kelmscott and Philip Webb, who had designed his first house, created a tombstone for him in a Cotswold tradition.

EDWARD BURNE-JONES *(1833-1898)*

Quentin Bell, writing in 1982, tells us that the Pre-Raphaelites were utterly unfashionable in the first forty years of the 20th Century (so much so that his parents, Clive and Vanessa Bell, leaders in the art world at the time, and many of their generation, could find nothing to say for any of the Pre-Raphaelites) but that by 1980 they could be considered a growth industry. With none of them is this more true than Burne-Jones. Not only is his work highly valued today, but he is seen as a precursor of some of the modern movements in art.[21]

He was born in Birmingham, the son of a picture-framer of Welsh origin, and his mother died soon after his birth. His childhood was very sad and confined, and he suffered much ill-health. In his isolation he took refuge in drawing. However at King Edward School he made friends and several of these went on to Oxford with him and remained friends for life. When he went up to Exeter College it was to study for Holy Orders. There he read widely and was influenced by the Romantic view of the Middle Ages and by the High Church Movement. His momentous meeting at Exeter was with William Morris. They read Ruskin and discovered his enthusiasm for the early Pre-Raphaelites, Millais, Holman Hunt and Rossetti, and, after a holiday visiting French Cathedrals, they decided to abandon thought of ordination and become artists. Burne-Jones left college before taking his final examinations and settled in London to learn painting from Rossetti. When Morris also moved to London with Street's office, the friends shared lodgings in Bloomsbury. Burne-Jones was poor and needed to work for his living; Rossetti helped by recommendations. One of these was to Powells, the stained glass firm, and his early designs for them were very successful. Noteworthy among them is the *Life of St Frideswide* window in Christ Church Cathedral, Oxford, to which Rosalind Howard referred in her description of her first meeting with her husband George. Although designing stained glass was to be an important part of Burne-Jones's work, he was primarily a painter and contributed one of the murals to the Oxford Union project. He was accepted into the social and artistic circle of Little Holland House, became a friend of Watts, met George

Howard and visited Italy with two of his friends. There he was influenced by the painting of such Italian masters as Mantegna and Botticelli.

A year after Morris's marriage, Burne-Jones too married the sister of one of his school friends. Georgiana McDonald belonged to the remarkable family of a Methodist minister, Alice McDonald became the mother of Rudyard Kipling, Agnes married the painter, Sir Edward Poynter, and Louisa was the mother of the Prime Minister, Stanley Baldwin. There was an idea of building another house onto the Red House to enclose a quadrangle for the Jones family, but it soon proved financially impossible and they settled in London. Two children were born to them; Philip who became a painter, and Margaret who married John Mackail, Morris's biographer and whose daughter was Angela Thirkell, the novelist. In 1867 they settled at the Grange, Fulham and later took a country home at Rottingdean, on the Sussex coast.

Throughout his life Burne-Jones was in frequent, sometimes daily, contact with Morris. Many artistic enterprises they had in common, including SPAB, but he never entered into Morris's socialism. 'I shall always deplore it', he said, for he felt it took his attention from his artistic pursuits. However, he was in general agreement with his social and anti-Imperialist views.

Burne-Jones took an active part in the decoration of the Red House and was one of the original partners in the Firm. More and more he became its principal designer. Not only did he create hundreds of figure designs and subject panels for stained glass, but also designs for embroidery, tiles and sculpture. When Morris's interest turned to printing, his contribution was immense, providing wonderful illustrative designs for woodcuts. For the great Kelmscott *Chaucer* he designed 87 woodcuts.

Burne-Jones always regarded painting as his real work. Indeed his stained glass designs were often done in an evening with surprising rapidity. In his later years he tended to paint huge canvases with romantic subjects from classical myth, Arthurian stories or allegory. Many of these were bought by well-to-do Northern businessmen, but they are now to be seen in galleries at home and abroad, especially in the United States. *Laus Veneris*, painted in the 1870s is now in the Laing Art Gallery in Newcastle upon Tyne. The most colourful of all his works, it portrays a queen with her maidens, lost in the contemplation of love.

Burne-Jones was a master, not only with pen and brush, but also of words. Though he published nothing, his whimsical and trenchant views are expressed with admirable felicity in Thomas Rooke's record published as Burne-Jones Talking, and in his letters. Another unexpected receptacle of his literary gifts is the account book, which recorded his dealings with the Firm. The theme of many entries is the poor reward paid by his 'employer' Mr Morris, and while they are delightfully humorous, one suspects they express a genuine feeling. Brampton provoked one of the best of these complaints and this is quoted in connection with the east window (above). Another entry is about his second commission for St Philip's Birmingham, now the Cathedral:

> It was in the year (I was about to say of Grace) 1885 that visiting my native city of Birmingham I was so struck with admiration at one of my works in St Philip's Church – (may I mention parenthetically that in that very church at the tender age of a few weeks I was enlisted amongst the rank and file of the church militant) struck with admiration at my own work (a naive confession which all artists will condone) I undertook in a moment of enthusiasm to fill the windows on either side with compositions which I hoped to make worthy of my former achievement. In the glow of the moment, carried out of myself with a sort of rapture, and as it were defenceless against the shafts of the avaricious and the mercantile I made no pecuniary stipulation. My thoughts, if not my actual words were 'I am in Mr Morris's hands – in the hands that is of an old and tried friend – he will see that my wife and children shall not suffer – he will take care that my old age shall not be embarrassed nor my good name tarnished by the offer of any inadequate compensation.' In this assurance I toiled – the heat of summer, the chills of autumn, the gloom of incipient winter have seen me still at work. And to what result? To this result, that for the production of two immense designs pronounced by my own family and one or two intimate friends to be masterpieces marking the culmination of my powers, my wages have been assessed at a sum – a pittance so contemptible that the idea for one moment occurred to me to hand over the despicable amount for parochial distribution – an unworthy thought, wrung out of me by honest indignation which I immediately discarded. I have done my work – I have learned a lesson for which I did not stipulate, and for which I tender my thanks to the Firm… To two cartoons for Birmingham £200 each… £400'.

Like his friends, Burne-Jones was opposed to the artistic establishment represented by the Royal Academy and he generally exhibited at the Grosvenor Gallery.

However, he eventually accepted Associateship of the RA, but exhibited only once, and resigned after a few years. Four years before his death he was made a baronet and after his death a Memorial Service in Westminster Abbey was the first held there for an artist.

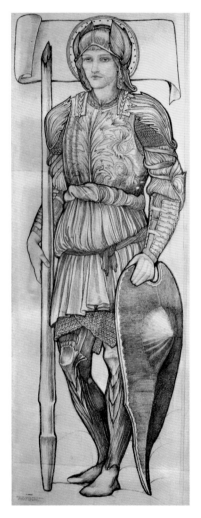

The cartoon for St George by Burne-Jones and the final figure as it appears in the east window

Noah
Window 1

NOTES & REFERENCES

1 David Harrison: *Along Hadrian's Wall*, 1956. In a subsequent edition he moderated his views, though a yet later paperback edition reverted to the dark and lurid judgement.

2 *Poems of Peter Burn*: complete revised edn London 1900, p100

3 A glacial feature which rises, surmounted by a motte, to the east of the town.

4 In about 1777 a baby had been born in Brampton to a member of a travelling theatrical company. She grew up to be the celebrated actress Harriot Mellon, who married the banker Thomas Coutts in his old age. Later still she married the Duke of St Albans. On Coutts's death she received the whole of his immense fortune, which she, in turn, left to one of his grandchildren Angela Burdett. Angela's charities were on a remarkable scale and included a number of churches and overseas cathedrals, including the now demolished St Stephen's, Carlisle. However, while it was, presumably, Harriot's Brampton origin which justified Routledge's application, it counted for nothing with Angela.

5 Charles Roberts: *Radical Countess*, 1962 p37

6 Rawnsley mistakenly says that the stone was laid by Princess Louise, Marchioness of Lorne, perhaps because, according to Penfold, she visited the church during its erection.

7 Roy Coad: *Laing*, 1979

8 Canon Rawnsley's verse ran:
Long may the tower that love has built so well
The memory of his unswerving spirit tell,
And every clock-beat only closer ring
The Christ he served to be your people's King.

9 Peter Cormack speculates that this was Ellen Mary Rope, 1855-1934, one of a family of artists. She made designs for reliefs manufactured by the Della Robbia Pottery at Birkenhead and specialised in friezes and panels depicting children as well as religious subjects.

10 Peter Burn: *Reminiscences of the late Rev Henry Whitehead – a Nonconformist's Tribute to a Churchman*, Carlisle, 1899

The chancel, showing the suspended upper vestry and the choir stalls

11 Canon HD Rawnsley, the joint founder of the National Trust and for many years vicar of Crosthwaite, published a biography of Whitehead in 1898, and the following year Peter Burn published a forty-page booklet – Reminiscences of the late Rev Henry Whitehead, a Non Conformist's Tribute to a Churchman, Carlisle, 1890.

12 A copy was presented to St Martin's Church some years ago.

13 Roberts: The Radical Countess, p156

14 Lethaby: Philip Webb and his work, p18

15 Pioneers of Modern Design, 1960

16 Lethaby op cit, p3

17 Lethaby op cit, p243

18 WR Lethaby contributed a series of articles on Webb to The Builder in 1925 and these were published in book form in 1935 after his death. A new edition, with additions, was published in 1979.

19 Edited by Briggs: William Morris – Selected writings and designs

20 Pioneers of Modern Design, p22

21 Parry: William Morris Textiles, 1983

22 Quentin Bell: A New and Noble School, 1982

BIBLIOGRAPHY

Much of the information contained in this account is drawn from documentation in the possession of the church or in the church documents held in the Cumbria Record Office at Carlisle. Philip Webb's Letter Book in the possession of Mr John Brandon Jones has provided additional information, as have documents among the Howard Papers in the care of the University of Durham. AC Sewter's monumental and authoritative *Stained Glass of William Morris and his Circle* includes much essential information including details of almost all Morris windows and their designs. Since the publication of the first edition of this book on St Martin's two very important works have appeared on the subject. First was Fiona McCarthy's biography in 1994. Then in 2005 came Sheila Kirk's great book on Webb which gives considerable coverage to St Martin's.

Barrie and Wendy Armstrong *The Arts and Crafts Movement in the North West of England* Oblong 2005

(Ed) Asa Briggs *William Morris: Selected Writings* Pelican 1962

Peter Burn *Poems of Peter Burn* complete revised edn, London 1900

Peter Burn *Reminiscences of the late Rev Henry Whitehead* Carlisle 1899

Penelope Fitzgerald *Edward Burne-Jones* Michael Joseph 1975

Martin Harrison and Bill Waters *Burne-Jones* Barrie and Jenkins 1973

Philip Henderson *William Morris, his life, work and friends* New York 1967

(Ed) Mary Lago *Burne-Jones Talking* John Murray 1981

WR Lethaby *Philip Webb and his work* OUP 1935, reprinted with additions by the Raven Oak Press 1979

Fiona McCarthy *William Morris: A Life for our Time* London 1994

(Ed) Gillian Naylor *William Morris by himself: Designs and Writings* New York 1988

Linda Parry *William Morris Textiles* 1983

Nikolaus Pevsner *Pioneers of Modern Design* 1960

HD Rawnsley *Henry Whitehead 1825-1896: A Memorial Sketch* 1898

Charles Roberts *The Radical Countess* Steel Bros, Carlisle 1962

AC Sewter *Stained Glass of William Morris and his Circle* (2 Volumes) Yale University Press 1974/5

EP Thompson *William Morris: Romantic to Revolutionary* Lawrence and Wishart 1955; revised 2nd edn New York, Pantheon, 1976

Paul Thompson *The Work of William Morris* Oxford 1967; 3rd edn 1991

APPENDIX

In an attempt to identify the many designs used by the Firm, AC Sewter devised a system of numbering, using the initials of the artist followed by a number. He explains that the basis of this system was an index of photographic negatives used by HC Marillier, the last managing director of the firm. The numbers have no chronological significance. The subjects of the designs used in the Brampton windows are listed below with these numbers.

Window 1

Adam BJ 312   Enoch BJ 143
Noah BJ 173   Abraham BJ 174
The Fall BJ 320

Window 2

Moses BJ 70   Solomon BJ 195
David BJ 191   Elijah BJ 144

Window 3

St John Evangelist BJ 19
St Peter BJ 24   St Luke BJ 17
St Paul BJ 71   Annunciation BJ 6

Window 6 (east window)

Angels with instruments BJ 393-4-5-6,
Angels with scrolls BJ 403-4-5-6-7
Christ as Good Shepherd BJ 399
St Martin BJ 398,
The Virgin Mary BJ 401,
Pelican BJ 402   St Dorothy BJ 400
St George BJ 397

Window 7

Hope BJ 147   Charity BJ 149
Faith BJ 148

Window 8

Elizabeth and John Baptist BJ 301
Salome with James and John BJ 303

Window 9

Christ blessing children BJ 492

Window 10

Timothy and Eunice BJ 300
Holy Family BJ 302

Window 11

Samuel and Eli BJ 105

Window 12

Reception of souls into Paradise
BJ 141

Angels with long trumpets BJ 26-27

Angels with scrolls adapted from
BJ 508

Window 13

Isaiah BJ 266   Ezekiel BJ 267

Window 14

Jeremiah BJ 268   Daniel BJ 269

Windows 4 and 5
No numbers given

ACKNOWLEDGEMENTS

I would like to acknowledge the kind permission of the following for brief extracts from the books mentioned:

Lord Briggs: *William Morris: Selected Writings and Designs*; Edward England Books: Roy Coad *Laing*; Faber and Faber Ltd: Nikolaus Pevsner *Pioneers of Modern Design*; Longmans Group UK: Philip Henderson *Letters of William Morris to his Family and Friends*; Mrs Joanna Matthews: Charles Roberts *The Radical Countess*; George Weidenfeld and Nicholson Ltd: Linda Parry *William Morris Textiles*; Yale University Press: Charles Sewter *The Stained Glass of William Morris and his Circle*; The Penguin Group: Nikolaus Pevsner: *The Buildings of England – Cumberland and Westmorland* (Penguin Books 1967) © Nikolaus Pevsner 1967.

Additional illustrations are by courtesy of:

The William Morris Gallery, Walthamstow
National Portrait Gallery, London, *p71 and p77 – images cropped and tinted*
Carlisle City Art Gallery and Museum
The Rector of Brampton, the Revd Averyl Bradbrook
Mrs LR Hopkins

Additional photography of the windows by the Revd Gordon Plumb

I am also grateful for the help of the Durham University Department of Palaeography and Diplomatic for access to the Howard Papers, to the Cumbria Records Office and St Martin's Church, Brampton for access to the church archives, to Mr Peter Cormack and Mrs Christine Boyce, who made valuable suggestions and to Mr John Brandon-Jones for permission to use Philip Webb's manuscript letter book, in his possession.

Having put everything in place for the
publication of this new edition of his work,
Arthur Penn died on 26 February 2008.
It is the wish of everyone involved in its
subsequent production that it should be a
fitting tribute to a dedicated scholar and
enthusiast of stained glass who truly loved
the Brampton windows.